wild by
nature

wild by nature

From Siberia to Australia,
three years alone
in the wilderness on foot

sarah marquis

ALLEN&UNWIN

First published in Great Britain in 2016 by Allen & Unwin

First published in English in the United States in 2016 by Thomas Dunne Books, an imprint of St. Martin's Press

First published in France in 2014 under the title *Sauvage Pour Nature: 3 ans de marche extreme en solidaire de Sibérie en Australie* by Éditions Michel Lafon

Allen & Unwin
c/o Atlantic Books
Ormond House
26–27 Boswell Street
London WC1N 3JZ
Phone: 020 7269 1610
Fax: 020 7430 0916
Email: UK@allenandunwin.com
Web: www.allenandunwin.co.uk

A CIP catalogue record for this book is available from the British Library.

Trade paperback ISBN 978 1 76029 072 6
E-Book ISBN 978 1 95253 418 8

Printed in Great Britain by Ashford Colour Press Ltd

10 9 8 7 6 5 4 3 2 1

To my dog, D'Joe, who gave me so much

To all the women throughout the world
who are still fighting for their freedom

Contents

wild by nature

Introduction

I'm back in the Swiss Alps after three years away, and everything is pretty much as it was, on the surface. I, myself—adventurer, woman, companion, daughter, sister, speaker, friend—am finding my place again in the scenery. My daily life is surprising, even exciting. I'm beginning to readjust to my old life, but things are different. In fact, nothing is as it was before. To start with, I've just survived three years of tumultuous adventures. And, believe me, this detail was not a foregone conclusion.

Today, I don't recognize the rhythm of my pen squeaking on paper as I attempt to faithfully capture the phrases that tumble through my head. My memory won't seem to unwind all the way; it feels like my whole being doesn't really want to remember. It's as though I've been forever marked by the hostile regions I crossed step by step, disguised as a man. There were so many nights when I fell asleep with danger prowling nearby. I could only ask my "guardian angel" for protection. In those moments, I forced myself to swallow high doses of positive thoughts, leaving no room for negative thinking. It was my only weapon. Today, like a wild fawn, I continue to slip into the scenery as I've habitually done for the past three years. I still have survival instincts that emerge in my daily gestures. It's like I have a huge tattoo, from three years of walking on my body, in my spirit, on my heart. I can't erase or hide it. This is how I am now.

Here, everything is so comfortable. Water comes out of the faucet, the fridge is full of good things to eat, and I even have an automatic coffee machine. I lift my eyes from my writing and move toward the coffeemaker, anxious to hear it purr.

I never asked myself how I would do it. What I felt at the deepest level was a sensation so strong that it became self-evident. I was going to become an adventurer.

So many steps—so many adventures—were needed to answer the single question: Why do I walk? The explanation is so simple as to be almost logical, pragmatic. It's enough to make me wonder if all these years, all these steps were really necessary to arrive at this understanding. And still, I can't help but think they were. I smile in recalling these years, having followed the signs of destiny all this time.

It's only in looking back through my wide-angle lens that I come to perceive these signs, to understand them, to feel them. The farther away I get, the more I see. It's why I never feel alone. My life until this point has been a mix of excitement, sweat, pure adventure, wild creatures with unpronounceable

Latin names, hairy, bare chests where I rested my head for an instant—all mixed with enough danger to keep me alert. This existence has also been full of choices. I won't be able to get everything down on paper, and yet, especially for women, I would like to record all of it, so as to leave a testament that tells of freedom, the freedom to choose one's life.

The story that follows is my story. I dedicate it to all of the women throughout the world who still fight for their freedom and to those who have gained it, but don't use it.

Put on your shoes. We're going walking.

1. Preparation

Before a departure . . .

"I wanted to be alone on my walk, but not just that.
My mission was both much more serious and at the
same time unique."

A SUBLIME SENSATION STARTED GROWING IN ME THE MO-
MENT that leaving showed itself to be the only option. I knew
deep in my heart that this departure was the only way to be
loyal to the fire that burned within me. I could feel it weakening,
the flame was shrinking. . . . It was time to go out and collect
the wood that would allow me to rediscover my life's flame.

That's how I left. On foot—a fact that presented itself to me as
obvious—and alone.

Don't misunderstand me. I didn't one day just jump in an

airplane, thinking, "Cool, I'm going to cross the globe walking from north to south!"

It required a huge undertaking, with tons of determination and energy, all before even beginning to walk. I had to put together a team that I could count on, with an expedition leader. For my two previous expeditions, my brother Joël had been by my side. Sabrina, his partner, had taken care of all the logistics for the "Path of the Andes" expedition. We planned everything over coffee, with no headaches, laughing as we went, sharing love for a job well done. After my last expedition, Joël set down his suitcases with his partner and their young daughter. He started his own mountain excursion business,[1] to which he devotes all his time. So I knew that this expedition would take place without him.

My twenty years of experience in this field has taught me that it's vital to anticipate any and all potential problems. I therefore set out to find someone living in each of the countries I was going to cross who could speak English and who, in case of an emergency, could organize an evacuation, talk with the authorities, take care of visas, etc.

In discussing preparations, it's important to take stock of the complexity of the project. In total: six countries to cross, diverse and varied terrain ranging from jungle to desert, from hot to cold, from snow to sand. As is my habit, I don't leave without equipping myself with good old topographic maps on paper, essential in my eyes. My new expedition leader suggests digital

---

1. You can find him at www.verbier-excursions.ch.

maps, which would have the advantage of being lighter. Something to keep in mind, maybe as plan B.

These operations have a cost that I have to determine and budget for in order to move on to the next step: finding partners to sponsor my expedition, which I've baptized eXplorAsia. At the same time, I need to devote myself to my physical preparation with an intense training program aimed at endurance.

And there it is, two years of preparation in a nutshell. Alone, I launched the machine of this gigantic initiative. As time progressed, good people appeared, as well as some who were not so good. Then one day we got the definite go-ahead. I could finally shift from the planning to the active phase of my expedition.

Vevey, Switzerland, June 2010— one week before departure

It's only three o'clock in the afternoon, but I'm exhausted. I lie down on my dog's bed, sharing it with him. I'm sad. I'm going to have to leave D'Joe in Switzerland. Each time my eyes fall on his wild coat flecked with red, white, and blue-grey, I can feel Australia, and it reminds me of our crazy adventures— the fire from which he saved my life, our long days without food, our stiflingly hot desert crossings, and our night walks when he wanted nothing more than to sleep. . . .

His breed is the closest a dog gets to a dingo. D'Joe is a Red Heeler, or Australian cattle dog. I saved his life on a farm when he was about seven.

This happened during my expedition to Australia, from 2002 to 2003, when I walked 8,700 miles—6,200 of them in D'Joe's company—across the most isolated zones on the continent. When we met, I made him a backpack and he became part of my life. Since then, we've shared everything. It seemed completely natural when D'Joe touched Swiss earth in the winter of 2003, after a remarkable flight. With no money, I had to call on people who had supported me from the beginning to fund the transport and quarantine costs of my loyal companion. *I can never thank those of you who repatriated D'Joe enough for your generosity.*

My heart tightens. I can't imagine not seeing D'Joe upon returning home. I've organized everything, even made appointments with a veterinary osteopath for his achy hind legs. I'll leave my scent in my room with clothes that I've worn; that way he'll sense my presence and won't worry, for awhile at least. I'm sad.

Eight days before I leave and my twenty-four-by-twelve-foot living room is full of gear. There's not an inch of floor that isn't covered in stuff, things piled on top of each other. I've meticulously planned each of my hypothetical needs. The store Yosemite in Lausanne helped me by taking charge of, among other things, the logistics of ordering gear. This is how I spent entire mornings with Alain and Sabrina, who were a huge help when it came to choosing all the equipment. My biggest concern was choosing the right footwear. Since the shoe company Raichle no longer makes the ones I've used for years, I had to choose another kind. The good old Swiss brand I wanted was sold out and my favorite model disappeared from the catalog. Let's hope my feet like my new walking shoes—I bought eight pairs.

That week, I only sleep a few hours.

I feel a mix of joy and dispiritedness. Sadness gnawing my stomach, I look at D'Joe lying on the pile of camping stoves and fleece jackets in the middle of the living room. Silently he says, "Don't leave . . . please," with eyes even sadder than mine.

But suddenly my mom, who joined the base camp at Vevey to give us a hand, slips on my backpack, which is way too big for her, and starts pushing my cart. Laughter ensues and lightens the mood. Meanwhile, Gregory, the expedition leader, is in the yard making sure that the satellite phone connection works with the solar panel.

A woman in Mongolia (preparation)

Each culture is a sort of magic box where one discovers with wonder and curiosity the habits and customs of a country. To survive in a foreign country, the first thing you need to do is learn about its history; I immersed myself in Mongolia's. And knowing that, generally speaking, only seven percent of the communication between two humans is based on language, I have a ninety-three percent chance that everything will go well. In Mongolia, the power of both the close and distant family clan is the key to everyone's survival, and the notions of property and privacy are less rigid than they are in the Western world. What outsiders might consider stealing, Mongolians would look at as being appropriate behavior within a family clan. *It's part of their identity*, something that is most likely why, for centuries, outsiders have viewed Mongolians as thieves.

In my backpack nestles an English-Mongolian dictionary, small and light, as well as my trusty collection of images that allow me to make myself understood. It contains illustrations of just about any basic situation—whether tense, dangerous, or funny—that a tourist might encounter in a foreign country; a white, female tourist, that is, one traveling alone in the steppe.

The Mongolian Cyrillic alphabet is related to an earlier Uyghur script. Learning the Cyrillic alphabet is, therefore, essential if you want to decipher Mongolian—the language of all of my topographic maps. Fortunately, the metric equivalents are the same as what I'm used to.

On the ground, I've used my ears a lot, asking locals I passed on my routes to repeat the names of the next villages, listening closely to the exact pronunciation. Then I'd repeat them over and over until I mastered the right intonation. Having evolved amidst so many different cultures, I know that a language isn't made of words; it has its melody, its intonations, its own rhythms that must be carefully observed.

Mongolia is one of the rare countries where my safety would be threatened just about every day. A country where the World Health Organization inventoried "diphtheria, hepatitis A, typhoid, Japanese encephalitis, pneumonia, tuberculosis . . ." and the list went on. Illnesses like the plague and brucellosis are still present in the steppe. Mongolia has also seen epidemics of meningitis and cholera.

My last vaccine was twenty years ago. It made me so sick that I never had another. But for this trip I had decided to get my tetanus booster, which I did, and also to protect myself against rabies. But this immunization required three injections given at fairly long intervals, and in the stress of my departure I hadn't had enough time. I was therefore well-advised to avoid being bitten or licked by a wild animal or a dog.

The preparations for my trip lasted two years and were tedious. Emptied, exhausted, I am finally sitting on the plane, seat 24B, ready to take off for Mongolia.

2. Mongolia, My Beginning

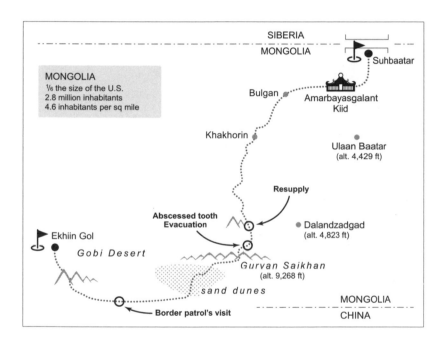

MONGOLIA
1/6 the size of the U.S.
2.8 million inhabitants
4.6 inhabitants per sq mile

SIBERIA
MONGOLIA
Suhbaatar
Bulgan
Amarbayasgalant Kiid
Khakhorin
Ulaan Baatar
(alt. 4,429 ft)
Resupply
Abscessed tooth Evacuation
Dalandzadgad
(alt. 4,823 ft)
Ekhiin Gol
Gobi Desert
Gurvan Saikhan
(alt. 9,268 ft)
sand dunes
MONGOLIA
CHINA
Border patrol's visit

I'M FORCED TO STOP, THE TEMPERATURE HAS AGAIN reached 104°F. My body has been reacting badly since the beginning and I need to listen attentively to what it has to tell me. I slow down and moderate my efforts.

On this day, I decide to walk to the thicket of trees I see from on top of a hill. It will take me more than an hour to reach this little zone of shade. Once there, I close my eyes and collapse, my head in my hands. It feels like there's a little monkey in my head, banging on metal cups. I know exactly what's happening to me, since it's what always happens to me at the beginning of an expedition. I've gotten sunstroke again, and yet, not an inch of my skin is exposed to the sun.

The next morning, I begin my day with my head looking like a slowly roasted pear. The morning light hurts my eyes, but I'm happy, the sunstroke has passed. At least that's over with!

I walk slowly, pushing my cart along the uneven terrain. This takes a lot of effort, but I know that without the cart, I wouldn't be able to travel these long distances where there's nothing, not a single village where I can resupply. I have with me two weeks' worth of limited food rations and over twenty liters of water reserves. After just ten short minutes, I come upon the other side of the hill.

What an unexpected discovery! I take off my sunglasses to be sure I'm seeing clearly. Before me is a valley full of real trees, a forest dense with birch, and at their feet a carpet of green ferns. The place is magical, and I'm so astounded by its beauty that I get out my video camera. It's as though I've been transported to another country, far from the typical, bare steppe.

Video camera in hand, I film this woodland scene straight out of a fairy tale. Suddenly, I catch my breath, my elbows squeezed against my body to keep from moving. Something brown has appeared in the frame. My eyes widen as the thing comes closer. My God, I don't think he sees me! Without taking my eyes off him, I check to see that the little red "record" dot is lit up on the screen.

He moves forward again—this morning's light breeze is blowing in the opposite direction—I'm lucky. He continues with prudent steps, as though he senses danger without being able to discern what it is. But his desire to follow his path wins out. Just then he rushes forward, a few yards from my camera. I stand silently in disbelief, bubbling over on the inside. Then he bounds away between the ferns into the woods. For a moment more I can make out his bouncing hindquarters before disappearing deep into the forest.

It was a magnificent buck just a few years old, given that his antlers weren't very big. I'm left speechless. His caramel garb and big, black eyes are still floating before me and I have to blink to come back to my senses. The encounter leaves me awestruck and full of energy. It erases all the little corporeal memories, sending nonstop signals of pain. I push my cart, suddenly light as a feather, up the slope. I thank the vagabond of the woods, the cause of the sudden lightness.

While my body walks, pushes, carries my movable house, my spirit smiles and slips away into another forest during the summer of 2002 in the United States. I was walking the 2,650 miles of the Pacific Crest Trail, a path that goes from the Canadian border to the Mexican border.

It's the end of a long day of walking. I find myself in a forest of dark, humid pines, where a sense of chaos reigns. Trunks covered in green moss blanket the ground, others remain halfway suspended. A large granite rock that seems to come out of nowhere catches my eye. I move toward it and joyfully put down my pack.

At my feet, a deep stream with no current, opaquely black, imprisons the big rock that I saw from far away. I undress and slip into the cold water. If you move into water slowly, the body adapts and the sensation of cold is diminished. Without moving, I sink little by little until just my head is above water. It's a simple experience of abandon; I feel like I'm nothing more than a head at the surface of this black water; my body has disappeared, the cold water has put it to sleep. Suddenly, a movement draws my attention to the other side of the stream. My eyes open wide, I can't believe it! It's a magnificent stag! He moves forward slowly, freezes, listens, then, after a long moment, bounds ahead elegantly and soundlessly. He swims, a procedure at which he demonstrates astonishing mastery. I still haven't moved, the top of the water is a true mirror. These majestic woods seem to shift themselves to the surface without a body beneath them. The black, stagnant water accentuates this impression. With no fear, the stag passes right next to me. He reaches the bank just a few steps from my dry clothes, then disappears, bounding elegantly into the dark and humid forest.

Back in Mongolia, my shoulders are untouchable because they hurt so much. Just about every one of my muscles is swollen. Since my departure, my body has creaked into motion like an old steam locomotive slowly taking off.

I started training a year ago, but didn't push myself as much as I did for the previous expeditions. I was short on time, as the size of the project didn't leave me much time to spare.

So I promised myself I would be careful at first, and find my rhythm. I move forward slowly but surely, as pushing a 110-pound cart and carrying a 40-pound pack on my back requires some effort. Since the ground is uneven, progress is difficult.

I find myself on the summit of one of the hills that I'd seen to the north, bare but green. The air is very heavy. Moving my tongue across my lips reveals the tension in my body. I'm sweating. Salt is everywhere, the temperature is holding steady at 104°F and there's not a single tree or bush around to provide shade.

From this small height, I carefully observe the curves of the countryside. I need to find water, which has been an incredibly difficult task up to this point. My long career as a water hunter spares me the anguish that most people would normally feel in this kind of situation. Over the years, I've used and acquired different techniques for gathering water. Here are a few of them:

- Dig a hole in the earth and cover the opening with a plastic bag. Place a small stone in the middle (on the plastic). The temperature difference between day and night will create a condensation effect and water will collect.
- Another technique is to wrap a branch covered with as many leaves as possible in an air-tight plastic bag. It's best to use this technique when the sun is at its height. The leaves will begin to sweat (a sauna effect) and after a few hours you'll be able to collect the condensation at the bottom of the bag.
- The third technique is ancestral and is also used by animals. In the dried-up bed of a sandy stream, you can sometimes find water beneath the soft surface. First, picture the streambed before you filled with water. Then look for a curve, or an obstacle like a big rock. This may be the place where the water was slowed down before the stream dried up. Once you've found such a spot, and you're sure that it's worth it to spend your energy and your sweat to dig a hole at least three feet deep, then start digging. Once you've accomplished your mission, take a nap. When you open your eyes, if you guessed right, you'll find a small quantity of water at the bottom of your hole.

There are lots of other techniques, but none of them result in the collection of more than a couple of ounces. It's imperative, though, to ask yourself the right questions before you start and to evaluate the quantity of water that will leave your body during the process of digging or setting the condensation trap.

Above all, I think it's not the technique that counts as much as your ability to read the landscape. All the clues are there, but you must empty your spirit of preconceptions, of theories. In 2006, I experienced an event that marked me forever and that helped me not only in my life as an explorer, but also in my life in general.

Water, where are you?

I was in South America on my Path of the Andes expedition, eight months of hiking on the cordillera. I was climbing a stony, difficult valley. Rough, grey rock dominated as far as my eyes could see. The wind, above all, was constant and wearing. I scanned the horizon looking for water, but in all this grey there was nothing that resembled life. I thought that if there was water, it would be accompanied by some form of life, logically vegetation. So I searched for green, or even just a simple change of color in the landscape, but there was nothing.

According to my topo map, a good-sized stream came in from the west and trickled into the valley that I was climbing going north. It wasn't the first time that my map announced streams that had turned into rock beds. I decided to stop and eat something. I knew that I would have to walk that day until I found water, and that I would need some energy. After a quick snack and a short nap, I decided to climb the sixteen-foot pile of rocks a few yards away. (Usually, I make it a point to get past any immediate obstacles before stopping or eating.) I put on my backpack and pushed to the summit, giving attention to the syn-chronization of my hands and feet. When I lifted my head, the spectacle before me took my breath away: a mountain stream, not very deep, but wide (just as it is on the map) was flowing vigorously. The lesson that I received that day is worth all of the lessons of survival. Why hadn't I seen this stream as I searched the horizon? I'd asked my spirit to look for green, thinking that it was what would lead me to water. Really? It did exactly what I had asked it to do. Except that at this altitude, there can be water and no vegetation (which is what I learned that day). I had made the greatest mistake!

I hadn't tried to read the terrain as it was before my eyes. Despite all my experience, that day I hadn't opened my spirit, I had sent it on a path that was based on a reflection, on a theory, an equivocation that came straight from my head. And yet, hadn't I felt the slight change in temperature caused by the presence of water?

The wall of stone created a real obstacle. And the wind alone camouflaged the sound of the water.

Sensitivity is the only answer for understanding a landscape. You must put aside logic, theories, good sense, and everything else. Blockages of the spirit are like imaginary barriers that we create for ourselves that prevent us from seeing.

This first day in Mongolia (continued) . . .

I notice a change in color a couple miles away, a darker shade of green, almost imperceptible in this very green green. An abnor-mal movement of the hills seems to break up the harmony of the countryside, the summits narrow, which could mean the presence of a small stream down below. The decision made, I throw myself into the descent. I take a narrow game trail, another indication of water, even if I haven't seen a single animal up to this point. I've drawn myself a small map to hold for reference, indicating the number of hills I have to climb before I get to those that seem greener. I'm consulting this small bit of paper when a melody reaches my ears. I turn, look around, but I'm unable to discern its origin. Suddenly, without having seen him come, there he is, sitting very straight on his horse, looking at me. The tune has stopped. My very first nomad is right in front of me. I smile, full of respect. I greet him. With no real expression on his face, he gives a very, very subtle movement of his head, looks at me an instant with the bit of paper in my hand, and decides to come and take it from me. His horse watches me intently as the man skillfully throws his leg over his saddle and plants his feet on the ground. He takes the paper from my hands, contemplates it, and squats down, lifting his traditional coat, as a woman would lift her skirt. I find this long, bottle green tunic-coat with its mandarin collar beautiful, and very practical. A single closure is located at the base of the collarbone, consisting of a series of cloth buttons. The garment is gathered at the waist by a large golden band that serves as a belt. He speaks only Mongolian, like nearly all the nomads who I'll meet after him. I pronounce the few words I've learned, among them the word for water, *us*, pronounced "ousse." On the ground, in the dust of the path, he begins to trace a crude map. Once finished, he marks with an X the spot where I'll be able to find water. Watching him, I find the same ease in his gestures that the Aborigines have when drawing in the sand. They're the only people I've ever seen who, after showing me my path, carefully destroy the sketch before leaving. I thank him a thousand times and use gestures to ask if I can take a picture. He motions for me to wait, swats the flies from his horse's eyes with the back of his hand, then checks that his tunic doesn't have too many wrinkles at the base of his belt. Now, he's ready for the picture. I show him the result on the digital screen. He looks at the screen with an indifferent eye. But the back and forth of his irises nestled between his taut eyelids reveals his excitement at seeing himself like that. With an agility inherited from his ancestors, he gets back on his horse without a word or gesture, and continues on his way. As soon as his horse finds its rhythm, the melody rises with the wind. I watch him move away into the distance, and I hop with joy. My first encounter was as beautiful as I could have imagined. I compose myself and decide to follow his instructions to the letter. Little time passes before a pretty mountain stream, completely hidden in the vegetation at the bottom of the valley, offers me its purity and coolness exactly where the nomad had indicated it would be.

The temple, the giant, and the infant

Now that I've finally found water, I can undertake the long climb that will have me cross a waterlogged forest of larches, positioned due north. The ground is damp, soaked with water, and the wheels of my cart sink into the mud. Pulling, pushing, sweating, slipping, after interminable hours of effort, I arrive on a berm. I read the ground like an open book: chewed bones, a pile of black ashes, ends of half-burned wood . . . people have eaten here, but it was well before the rains. I stop and make myself some tea with a few twigs that are more or less dry. Until now, I had to skip my tea breaks due to lack of water. Not anymore; my two ten-liter containers are now filled with crystal-clear water. Tea is much more than tea for the desert dweller that I am. It's a moment when I extract myself from reality by watching the dance of the flames and drinking this warm liquid.

I don't reach the summit until the next day. In front of me, in the middle of the forest, stands an immense cairn fifteen feet high, made of small stones carefully piled, mixed with blue scarves, wood, money, various objects, and broken bottles of vodka. I realize that I'm in the presence of an *ovoo*.

According to tradition, when you encounter an *ovoo* on your path, you must stop and walk three times around it clockwise, adding another stone each time you go around. The traveler can then continue on, knowing that he is protected. He can, if he wishes, leave offerings in the form of candy, money, milk, or vodka.

Mongolians are animist. Animism is the conviction that all things possess their own spirit. Even today, Mongolians still worship the spirits of the sky, the mountains, water, and the moon, leaving them milk, vodka, or money offerings.

I carefully avoid this place out of respect and continue on my path. I hurry my steps, I must arrive at a temple which will be my first chance to resupply since my departure.

I can make out a faint path which, I imagine, will take me far from this forest, and I decide to follow it. The village must not be far away. In less than an hour, I'm already out of the forested zone and find myself, with great pleasure, surrounded by cows, horses, and sheep. I progress slowly while taking in what's around me. Far away, a man relaxes in the shade of a tree. The repetitive movement his horse makes to brush off the flies catches my eye. The nomad lying on the ground knows he's been spotted. He unhurriedly gets to his feet and settles into his saddle to catch up with me. After a "*sainbanou*,"[2] he invites me to his house for tea, which I gladly accept. We pass through a herd of sheep, and he accompanies me to his yurt, which is a few hundred yards away. A woman with wrinkled, copper-colored skin immediately comes out to meet me and invites me inside. I don't think she's more than fifty. She sports a bizarre fold of skin that hangs heavily over her skirt. Her sweater is too short, and it's as though her stomach is trying to crawl away. I lower my head and enter. The space is empty, rugs are scattered over the ground. I sit down as I should, without my feet sticking out in front of me, taking care to fold my legs beneath my body. I am sitting to the left of the central pillar, the place to the right of it being reserved for the head of the family, his wife, and his close family.

I immediately feel a wonderful sensation: I adore this round tent made of sheep felt. The woman makes me some tea and, with a frank smile, asks me to turn around. Which I do. A stifled exclamation escapes my throat, the kind that one makes before something bigger than anything, where the greatest mystery of life resides: a small baby is lying there, swaddled in protective cloths like a larva. Questions crowd my head. When was he born? He seems to be only a few days old. Where could she possibly have given birth? I wonder how and in what conditions Mongolian women traditionally give birth.

---

2. "Hello" in Mongolian.

Smiling, I congratulate her; she seems to understand. A dog appears in the door frame, looks at me, and leaves. He seems to say, "Everything's okay here, I'll check back again soon. 'Long Nose' would do well not to move an inch." Where the child has been placed on the ground, a ray of sunlight penetrating the opening at the top of the yurt gently caresses the infant. The woman serves me *suutei tsaï*, the famous tea made with salty milk. It's a bowl of milk that could be from a yak, a mare, a camel, or something else, to which is added a pinch of salt and a little tea. The tea is accompanied by a piece of something mysterious that resembles a bit of cheese but is as hard as a rock. I thank her and slip the morsel discretely into my pocket. In the steam of the tea, I perceive a rancid odor that assaults my nostrils before it even wets my lips. My stomach instantly contracts. I clench my teeth and I drink. (I'll later learn to appreciate this salty tea after spending months in these Mongolian lands.) I drink with little sips; she lifts her eyes from the steaming bowl and smiles timidly. We digest this moment in the company of her newborn, in the intimacy of silence.

It doesn't last as long as I would have liked; the distinct sound of a galloping horse rings out. On edge, the dog barks, the sheep stir. A man, then another, followed by a young man and a red-cheeked young woman arrive. Everyone sits down. They choose their seats precisely, and I'm able to determine who is family and who is just passing through. Suddenly, the red-cheeked young woman removes her undershirt, exposing her breasts to anyone who cares to look at them, not excluding any males present. The newborn's mother immediately lowers her gaze, as she sits on her heels, her legs carefully folded beneath her body. Her features fall, and a gentle rocking movement settles in. She seems angry and sad, the light is gone from her face.

A multitude of questions flood my mind and in my head I begin to lay out the problems that could follow from so public a display. I decide to draw away, respectfully taking my leave from the mother and offering her a reassuring smile. Without waiting for a response, I extricate myself from this atmosphere that has become unbreathable. A rumbling of words follows at my heel, as everyone exits the yurt except the mother. They scream at me, accompanied by some spitting here and there. It seems to be full of reprimands that I translate as, "You must stay and sleep here, live with us, eat with us and . . . take off your undershirt when we do!" But of course, I could be mistaken in my interpretation of this family drama!

My legs don't wait for an order to get far away from this place, as quickly and unobtrusively as possible. I can only smile with astonishment at what just happened.

"Ahhh . . . these Mongolians . . ." escapes my throat.

I take off toward the temple. The dog follows me a dozen yards behind; he seems to be telling me, "Don't be angry with them, they're just like that."

From far away, the temple imposes itself on the scenery like a guardian of the steppe. It's beautiful from here, with its large, red earth palisades and its roofs curved at the edges. All of the architecture of Asia is there, before my eyes. . . .

A man is working at the foot of the south wall. I'm just five hundred yards away. But from where I am, I can't quite tell if the man is tall or if the wall is gigantic.

I leave my pack at the entryway, ready for inspection by the dog that followed me, whose gentle eyes tell me of his empty belly. I pet and scratch him gently, and he smiles at me. Far away, the man who was digging stops, gets awkwardly to his feet, and leaves. I'm dumbfounded—he's a real giant, dressed in the traditional coat called a *deel*. All of this gives him an imposing appearance. He flees upon my arrival. He had been sitting on his bottom like a child, digging trenches for water drainage with a pickaxe. From far away, the pickax looked like a toothpick in his hands. Poor guy, he must have been worried that I would take his picture. I'm sad for him, and angry at tourists who steal photographs without permission. A photograph should never be stolen. It's a moment in time, a life, an instant, that the picture freezes. There's responsibility in it.

I enter the courtyard where everything seems to be falling into ruin. Bags of sand are scattered over the ground, there are piles of brick strewn about, plastic bags vibrate in the wind. In a corner, a scaffolding seems to belong to a colony of pigeons who've taken up residence. I leave immediately and run into the young woman from the yurt who gives me a fake smile. Like her dog, she starts following me and yelling "money." As she makes her demand, she gives me a look that I don't know how to describe: Her eyes are stuck between her unblinking eyelids, her expression seems frozen on her face. I can't figure out how to read these people, they all seem to have the same frozen expression. Their expressions are so minimal, I'm going to have to figure out how to do things differently in the future.

She struggles to keep up; my sustained walking speed exasperates her and she grumbles behind me. My stomach is emitting strange sounds. I stop an instant and look behind me. She's let me go and turned around to go home, her dog at her heels.

I progress in the direction of the yurts that I see far away. I cross the river without difficulty, as it's not very deep. I approach the fence encircling a series of perfectly aligned yurts. They seem too well aligned, and there's no sign or emblem.

Two young girls come out to meet me, and look at me strangely. It might be because I'm streaked with mud and I haven't washed since . . . well, since I left, twelve days ago!

To my great surprise, I've just found one of the first Mongolian tourist camps. I smile a lot, too much, I think, for their taste. I've noticed so little expression on their faces. No smiles, either. I wonder if this has something to do with the well-known Asian cultural value of "saving face, no matter what the situation." I count around thirty yurts, but there's no one there, not a single tourist. They ask me for money. I pay the fee, which seems appropriate. We exchange niceties thanks to my little translation book, and they ask me the following questions: "How old are you? Where is your husband?"

I'm tired, I'm hungry, I need to eat, to resupply, can't they understand? I start gesticulating. . . . Eureka, they bring me a bowl of boiled mutton swimming in hot milk, which emits such a distinctive odor.

I take a deep breath, keep smiling, and try to explain that I don't eat sheep. I shout, I gesture, I'm my own traveling theater. But despite rolling out all my artistic talents, they remain indifferent, with their narrow eyes and their stoic expression (that would irritate me so many times). At that moment one of the girls steps back, looking terrified. No? It's not possible, I think. I need to test my intuition, so once again I open my eyes very wide! Poor thing, she really looks scared! What does she imagine I am? A double cyclops dragon from the north?

I think I must be the only "Big Eyes, Long Nose" that she's

ever seen. This makes everyone laugh. One of the girls laughs so hard she has to leave to urinate, but she doesn't go too far, just to the right of the yurt's doorway. I entertain this little world for a bit longer, then notice that my stomach almost aches. I leave and head to my yurt. The girl who had left to pee catches up to me. I notice that she sped up using a technique of casual-looking speed-walking where the arms swing alongside the body while taking tiny, rapid mouse steps and scuffing her feet along the ground. I've seen so many women on the Asian continent run in this manner (a technique that the Japanese in particular seem to have mastered).

She opens the door of what I'm going to call "my yurt" and squats in front of the central hearth. She gets to work lighting a little fire in the tiny square stove made of corrugated metal that's in the middle of the dwelling. The interior fascinates me; I adore this structure. It's highly soundproof; the wind seems to politely stop at the door, which I appreciate. It's truly a peaceful harbor. She leaves, and I collapse with exhaustion on the bed near the fire. Not long afterward, a sensation of urgency that I know well awakens me. I slip on my shoes and run quickly toward the equivalent of the restrooms. The famous, the fabulous, the incredible Mongolian tea with salted milk has set off a gastric tsunami. As I leave the outhouse, I discover what seems to be a shower. I do a little test; a small trickle flows from a hose then becomes a drip, but the most important thing for me is that this water is warm. I return to my yurt, cut the top off an old liter-and-a-half bottle, and collect the water patiently, washing a little at a time and ending with my hair. . . . Two hours later, rid of salt on my skin, I feel better. I return to my yurt, and they bring me a plate of white rice with an egg. My God! Incredible! *Thank you, thank you.* .

Life couldn't be more beautiful than it is at this exact moment. I eat at a speed that impresses even me. I could easily have eaten three plates like it. I want to sleep and not think anymore, not try to communicate, just sleep.

In my head, I recap: I broke all recommendations—don't eat dairy products, don't touch animals. . . . But hey, I saw a giant! I smile and, with these last thoughts, I fall asleep next to the fire. It feels so good.

Some minutes later, I'm awakened by claps of thunder. I open the door of the yurt and look outside. The sky has metamorphosed into an enormous, swollen black cloud; the air is heavy and taut. At the same moment, far away, a series of lightning bolts tear in unison at the horizon. I run out quickly to capture these puffed-up, menacing clouds before it begins to rain. The girl reappears, worried; she puts out my fire and pulls out my chimney, placing the rolled-up tube of corrugated metal in the middle of my yurt. Just then, the sky officially falls to Earth. My yurt is barely touched by what's happening outside: I shut my eyes, safe for the night.

Weeks later . . .

I'm exhausted. Again last night I endured an invasion of night riders into my camp.

I've hardly spent a peaceful night without intrusion since I set out. From the moment daylight erases itself from the western sky, fear rises and sleep won't come—the sleep I religiously depend upon to recuperate.

Men on horseback have taken to visiting me at twilight. Like wolves, they move about when night falls, gliding through the shadows until they arrive at my camp. I never hear them before they've arrived.

The steppe is bare, without any sort of natural shelter. There's not a tree, not a depression in the ground, the grass is overgrazed, and the wind whips through at any hour of day or night. I'm in the middle of nowhere, far from villages. And still there are these night horsemen. . . .

The wind blew hard this morning. Taking in my surroundings, everything is green for miles around. Far away I see a crude shelter for sheep. I decide to change direction to take refuge in this structure so basic that one would think it was a child's fort. I arrive, letting my pack fall to the ground and myself with it. I have to sleep, I'm completely spent. I close my eyes and instantly fall into a deep sleep.

Hours later, a small sound penetrates my slumber. A faint repetitive noise. My body is still in the same position in which I collapsed. I'm comatose, still half asleep, burrowed in my Gore-Tex jacket, a warm hat pulled snugly over my head. I feel so good, I don't want to move. I'm worn out. The first month was incredibly hard, I have the taste of constant effort in my mouth, and my whole body hurts. . . . Suddenly, I sense that something is happening and I open my eyes.

There she is, right in front of me. She lifts her head and stares at me a moment, as though she knew that I wasn't one of the furry four-leggeds that she was used to seeing here. Then she goes on about her business, at regular intervals poking her long, curved beak into the earth. She continues her work, glancing at me quizzically from time to time, apparently not seeing me as a danger.

My eyes are glued wide open. I avoid any movement and stifle a shout of joy that feels as though it comes from far away, rising up through years layered upon years. *As a child, I was fascinated by nature's rhythm and her inhabitants. A passion for ornithology came naturally to me. For my eighth birthday, my parents bought me a complete guide to European birds. I spent whole seasons, summer and winter alike, in the forest, watching without moving, with heavy binoculars, in the hopes of seeing one particular bird. Its image was on the cover of the field guide. Its salmon color, spotted with black and white, gave it an exotic air. Its crest and gently curved beak seduced me from first glance.* I'm fascinated, I can't believe my eyes. Tears roll down my cheeks, tears of joy. I've just lived my most cherished childhood dream: seeing the hoopoe bird.

3. Central Mongolia

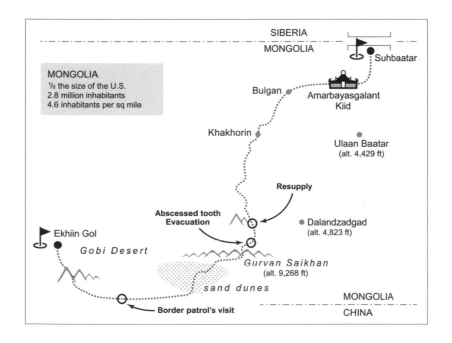

MONGOLIA
⅛ the size of the U.S.
2.8 million inhabitants
4.6 inhabitants per sq mile

SIBERIA

MONGOLIA

Suhbaatar

Bulgan

Amarbayasgalant
Kiid

Khakhorin

Ulaan Baatar
(alt. 4,429 ft)

Resupply

**Abscessed tooth
Evacuation**

Dalandzadgad
(alt. 4,823 ft)

Ekhiin Gol

Gobi Desert

Gurvan Saikhan
(alt. 9,268 ft)

sand dunes

MONGOLIA

Border patrol's visit

CHINA

Large raptors take off and alight in precise spots, barely beneath the lip of the mountain pass I've just climbed through. I observe them. They're magnificent, using the thermal stream with mastery and without apparent effort. Down below, permanent buildings appear. They look windburned, with little trace of the white paint they once wore. I enter this village from the north.

Dust is flying everywhere. The ground is made of light brown earth that time has rendered as hard as pavement. The wind continues tirelessly to attack all who find themselves in its way, leaving repetitive, strident sounds suspended in the air. This little village of two hundred souls will be composed of over five thousand people during the winter. Most nomads return here to camp with their yurts, which they surround with a board fence. For now I need water, my topo maps indicating no water source whatsoever for the next sixty miles. I absolutely must fill all my water containers here. It's all that I hope to find in this phantom village.

My legs keep their rhythm, the same as always. I move forward. The place seems dead, or really just lifeless, until voices reach my ears. I notice a woman eyeing me from afar before disappearing between two buildings. I progress down the village's only road. I stop my convoy in front of a structure whose door stands open. In accordance with Mongolian habit, there is no indicator, no sign, no emblem. I put down all my things outside and enter through this little wooden door, a faded emerald green. The door is composed of two panels, and I slip through the one that's open. Inside, a voluptuous woman is behind a counter. A few bottles of vodka are displayed on the single, long shelf. The woman ignores me, she's busy looking at herself in a small mirror. I greet her in her language and ask where I might find some water and the village market. She aggressively responds, "Vodka here!" and immediately disappears through a small door. I look behind the counter and see nothing but bottles of vodka, no faucet or spigot. I turn around. Dilapidated stools are planted in a corner of the room, the walls are falling into decrepitude, and it smells of musty oldness mixed with vomit. Even so, between these four walls, I'm protected from the wind's talons. This does me good, and I appreciate it. I go back outside to my things. To my great surprise, I find two fat Mongolians oozing alcohol in the process of extracting my meager possessions from my backpack. I shout at them sternly and snatch from their hands my GPS and my hat, which they've already appropriated.

"Where can I find water?"

They don't seem to understand, so I act it out, pretending to drink from my water bottle, turning it upside-down to show them that it's empty. Suddenly, I notice a long, rolled chimney on the roof of a building just behind me. The voice of my contact in Ulaanbaatar resonates in my head: "The public baths are the place where people wash. From time to time they heat them up and use them. You'll be able to spot them easily. It's the only building with a big chimney climbing into the sky."

I turn and look at these two characters and their dopey expressions.

I wave toward the public baths. They immediately bellow their reply of "*Barko!*"[3] Then they turn on their heels, certainly out of fear of having to help me, and go into the "bar" by the little door that looks too narrow for them. I stay right on their heels. The moment my foot crosses the threshold, the fat lady from behind the counter enters in a panic. In fact, I can clearly see that she's angry, her face becomes tomato red, and she paces back and forth behind the counter. I don't feel the need to know the translation of what she's yelling at me. . . . And that's how I got kicked out of my first illegal tavern like a mangy dog. So I leave. And now what do I do? I go back in, what else? I can't throw in the towel, this village is empty and the only people who can give me water are right there in front of me. Before anyone can move, I sit myself down between the two friendly chaps and order a round. Glasses are filled, I let the men drink and then, sweetly, I ask where I can find water. The woman understands my strategy and laughs as she asks me, "Another round?" lifting the bottle in her hand. I smile at this drunk woman, look at

---

3. "No" in Mongolian.

her associates who can barely stand up, and leave, slamming the door behind me.

Great, so what's plan B? With neither options nor inspiration, I head toward the door of the public baths. *Hmm.* A huge, rusty padlock holds fast the two panels of the iron door. There's no way I'll be able to force my way in. I walk around the building in case there's another access point. I'm getting antsy, this is making me angry. I need to get out of this place; I know that I'm not safe here, I can feel it. I turn around, worn out. This band of idiots has sucked all my energy. And now, I want to leave, to go far enough away that my camp is out of their reach, but the sun has already started to sink and I NEED WATER! Suddenly, the presence of a man who appears out of nowhere pulls me from my thoughts. He's standing there, just in front of my belongings, and gestures for me to give him my empty water containers. I hesitate. I'm scared he'll steal them from me. I examine him from behind my sunglasses. He's wearing traditional clothing, and he seems different. Do I have a choice? Not really . . . I decide to give him just one of my water containers. He returns five minutes later with my ten-liter reservoir full. He tells me to taste the water. It's beautiful, clean, sweet. I'm relieved. I hold out my other containers, he gives a quick smile and comes back soon after with the precious liquid. I don't know how to thank him, and take out my translation guide. With his two calloused hands, he gently closes the book and smiles at me without a word. I look at him and I understand. I attach the water containers on the underside of my cart between the two wheels, where the weight will cancel out. I don't have to beg for my legs to take me away from here, and I distance myself quickly.

Yet my curiosity is too strong, I turn around: He's still there in the middle of the road, he hasn't moved, he's watching me leave. I gaze at the horizon. In the interior of my being, a gentleness engulfs me: I just met one of my "protectors."

In the newfound silence, I smile; I'm deeply grateful.

Grains of sand beat against my left cheek, my eyes sting. I stop to wrap my head in a wide cotton square to protect myself from the wind.

The wind dehydrates, it burns. Paired with temperatures of over 100°F it can be fatal. It's an insidious gnawing that slowly, imperceptibly wears you down.

I lift my head and scan the horizon, which continues to undulate. Before me stretches what I would call a desert plain: nothing in common with the vast hills of the north. I turn around one last time and can just make out his silhouette between two blasts of dust, then in the time it takes to recover my face, he's disappeared.

My legs seem more than happy to put some miles between themselves and the village. They advance without effort. Between two gusts of sand, I'm able to make out rocky forma-tions, a bit to the west, and decide to go in this direction. I have to figure out a spot that's protected from the wind to put up my tent. In less than an hour, I find myself in the shade of a big, irregular sandstone rock formation. I take a break to consult my maps.

I have with me topographic maps edited by the Russians to a scale of 1:500,000; they date from the 1950s. And to round things out, I have three maps of the entirety of Mongolia. Not one of them, if I compare them, contains the same information. They're all more or less wrong or more or less right. So I read them with close attention, looking for any scrap of information that may have escaped me.

The spot is ideal, I can put up my tent sheltered from the wind. I look up from my maps dreamily, when suddenly a cloud of dust far away catches my eye. I get out my binoculars: I can barely make out the shapes of two horsemen on the horizon. I quickly pack up my maps and get back to walking. If they don't find me, they'll look for me. And I don't need them wondering where I'll stop for the night. Staying in motion will keep from tipping them off. I keep my walking rhythm, but the sandy ground slows me down and frankly, my day was already full enough. I just hope they'll go past me. The cloud of dust approaches gradually. I slow down, I'm so tired. I hear shouts. I don't even turn around. But here they are, entering my field of vision on the left. Oh God, no, not them! I manage to hide my emotion, showing no sign of my astonishment. It's the two drunk guys from the village. They're going on about I don't know what, each holding a bottle of vodka in his hand. I wonder how they stay on their horses. One of the two stooges decides to give me his bottle, with which he barely misses whacking me on the top of the head. "Alright, that's enough!" I yell at them in French, without success. They giggle, and do what they came to do: amuse themselves at a game of "steal the cart of the woman who walks." The wind is blowing hard, it's the end of the day. They move away a little and then come back just as fast, charging me at full speed with their horses, barely avoiding me at the last possible moment. Until now, I've stayed calm, but it's become clear I need to react, and fast. These two poor guys are starting to get on my nerves. I need to get control of the situation and take action.

"Don't you know, gentlemen, that you shouldn't push me too far when I'm tired?" This phrase has never come out of my mouth before, but I'm not scared, I'm ready. My eyes don't leave them, behind my sunglasses I instinctively look for an opening. I don't move. Standing still, focused, I observe them. . . . It's the only way to make my plan work. I look for the right moment to put it into action. A gust of sand comes up. Now!

Their horses are close enough, too close, I throw myself toward them all at once, arms in the air and screaming like a madwoman, with the goal of scaring them and throwing them off balance. The horses' reactions are immediate: they buck, shaking the two buffoons like children, who just manage to keep themselves from falling off. I hope that this merry-go-round has unsettled them, even if no one is hurt. My plan works perfectly. I was lucky that they were so drunk, as even a ten-year-old could have gotten back in the saddle in the same situation. They glare angrily, understanding that I'm not afraid. In a way, they lost face by almost falling off their horses. They depart without another word, and I watch them as they go. From behind, they look like two bulging babies as they disappear from my field of vision. The brown cream sand seems to have devoured them, which means that they can't see me anymore, either.

Good, that's done with!

All that activity gives me a good flood of adrenaline and I no longer feel tired. It's lucky, since I can't stay here for the night. I walk two hours more and find a winter shelter for livestock. Unfortunately, this shelter is too obvious; it's the first place those cretins or another member of their clan would look for me. I need to avoid their logic. So I continue until my cart rolls effortlessly on a solid surface. It's a hardened layer of sand that stretches for several hundred yards. I smile, it's just what I was waiting for. My cart won't leave any trace of my passage. I look all around, and notice nothing abnormal in the landscape. I slip quickly behind some rock formations and disappear. I park myself behind a rock and wait, listening. After fifteen minutes, with all still calm, I go deeper into the rock formations to find a camp that's protected from the wind that's picking up even more. Finding a spot that offers enough shelter takes thirty minutes. I put down my load and sink to the ground with an interminable sigh. Night has already fallen and I put up my tent in the dark, without my headlamp. I'll eat a cold dinner, nibbling raisins and dry Mongolian biscuits known as *bolsak*. Lighting my camp stove is out of the question. It's a clear night, the sky is full of stars. It's beautiful. I've survived another day! I smile and forget my difficult day beneath this ceiling of stars. Good night.

Upon waking up, I discover where I am with new eyes. Night has already allowed in some light. I put my teapot on my stove, finally! The events of the previous night no longer weigh on my spirit. Long ago I installed an "erase" button. Each day is a new day. I've forgotten yesterday on the surface, but not in my cellular memory. It's a little like deleting an image from your computer's desktop while it's still saved on the hard drive. The spirit works like that, in layers.

I'm not, in fact, completely awake. My body aches. Wrapped in my sleeping bag, holding my steaming cup of tea, I watch as dawn arrives.

This moment is mine. It's magical, indescribable. I feel so lucky. I need this space for myself. I also need to get going to take advantage of the coolness of the dawn, but I grant myself this moment, since it feeds me differently. My interior requires nourishment as much as the rest of me. It has everything to do with balance: the success of my expedition depends on all of these little daily details, on "being mindful in each moment." I so love these few minutes when Earth is waking up.

But I have to follow the only rule that I've written in stone: never spend more than one night in the same place (except in case of an emergency). I must always advance, one foot in front of the other. I take off my night clothes—pink leggings and a sky blue T-shirt—and slip into my adventurer's uniform, dirty and masculine. My night clothes are colorful and feminine, they make me smile, and it's important for my morale. My daytime clothes camouflage me with their sandy color, their smell, and most important, the fact that they're men's clothes. I fold up my camp and take my first steps, without looking too far ahead. It will take my body two hours to warm up and function without too much pain.

By four o'clock in the afternoon, I've already started looking for a place to camp for the night, but there's nothing on the horizon. The sound of a motorcycle coming from the south reaches my ears. The vehicle catches up to me, the motor stops.

When two travelers meet in the desert plains, it's natural for them to inform one another of the conditions that they'll encounter.

The guys on the motorcycle shake like dogs, dust flies

everywhere. I look them over from behind my sunglasses. The small, wiry one has scars on his face, mischief in his eyes, and is wearing jeans. He looks like a real delinquent. The driver is an ungainly Mongolian not unlike others I've seen, who, for the occasion, has lifted up his T-shirt to display his round belly. Oh no! Not another one who's going to pee right next to me! But to my great surprise, the man with the scars pulls something from the pocket of his jacket. It's a clear plastic bag full of marijuana. "How much do you want?" he asks. "No thanks, I don't want any." I speak without letting my surprise creep into my voice. He insists, I stand firm, the tone rises. He starts eyeing my gear while making little comments to his colleague. The air is suddenly charged with waves that say, "Get out of here! Now!" Without a word, but with conviction, I position my cart to leave and take a step. The reaction is immediate, I hear them spitting words in my direction. I keep moving. Suddenly, silence, I hear nothing. Then, without any doubt, a familiar sound reaches my ears. . . . They're peeing! I smile beneath my scarf; I would have bet a fortune that they were going to do it! I hear sounds that suggest getting back on the motorcycle, and as they start the motor, I still haven't turned around. I continue walking in the same rhythm.

Never give importance to people or animals whose attention you don't want to attract. To ignore is the best solution. To avoid provoking them, don't look at them frankly, but also don't give them a chance to look at you for too long. It's crucial to find a happy medium, a certain poise that gives off a sense of calm. Being scared won't serve you well under any circumstance, so you might as well strike this emotion from your list of options.

This is not to be confused with real fear, which we'll encounter later. . . .

At this point, the physical effort is brutal. I'm walking a lot, and I hurt all over! I film myself without knowing where the energy it takes to film will come from. I just feel like doing it.

Before leaving, I knew that it would be imperative—if this expedition was to nourish me—to suspend all judgment and hasty conclusions about what I would see and experience. Now I smile at my earlier innocence. . . . And I have yet to knock at the door of Asia.

It takes me five days to cross this plain, hiding myself carefully each night. I finally arrive at a place where I should be able to find water, according to my maps. I only have a liter and a half left, which I preciously keep in my sight, attached to one of the straps on my pack.

Tiny black, brown, and white dots appear on the slope of a rock. I smile. They're little Mongolian goats, used primarily for their prestigious wool, known as cashmere. Mongolia produces approximately 2,700 tons of it per year.

To protect themselves during the harsh winters, these little Hyrcus goats produce a fine down beneath their summer coat. A simple brushing in the spring is enough to collect as much as five ounces of precious down per goat. I've gotten to see several nomads in early summer loaded down with a mass of large, white bundles waiting endlessly on the side of a road for a truck that was headed to town. Often, they wait there until the end of Naadam, their independence day, and the wool diminishes in value. To the family, the only souvenirs it brings are a few bags of rice and sugar, some bricks of tea, and liver damage.

"In the summer we party, in the winter we sleep." Isn't that what my contact had told me?

Until meeting these ladies with the precious down, I'd never really wondered where cashmere came from.

I remember having traded my technical clothing for natural fiber on my expedition in South America. The temperature dropped to -4°F and the altitude left with me a constant icy shiver running the length of my bones. So I decided to do as the indigenous people, who didn't seem to suffer from the cold. I wore alpaca wool beneath my Gore-Tex jacket. My body temperature stabilized and the shivers disappeared. So it was as a matter of course that in Mongolia I tested, with great curiosity, yak wool (warm but itchy), camel wool nighttime socks (very comfortable and warm), and finally the cashmere hat I have to this day (perfect for heavy physical activity and sweating, as well as for cold). Our skin breathes, so I think it's beneficial to have it in contact with a natural material. I like the idea that by simply shearing or brushing their animals, these people can live off their livestock without having to kill them. I've used Icebreaker merino wool for years. This gesture creates a positive chain reaction for the animals (who aren't killed) and for the humans and their families.

Upon seeing the goats that day, I know that water can't be far away. I climb down from this windy, dry plateau on a path carved by these little goats to get to the flat area below. I throw myself into the descent, my eyes are glued to the green grass far ahead. This green looks almost artificial and contrasts starkly with the burnt brown of the rest of the plain that stretches as far away as my eyes can focus. Yurts are lined up at regular intervals along a good-sized stream. The alert is given, I know I've been spotted, and a small man comes galloping up. He's spinning a string in the air to which is attached a piece of wood ten inches long by an inch-and-a-half wide that's whacking the back end of the horse. The horse, however, doesn't seem to go any faster after getting smacked by the wooden thing. He stops and observes me, circling around me. Another little fleabag, as I affectionately call them. This man is very thin and reminds me of a street kid. His eyes are dark and hard; his childhood seems far behind him despite his ten years. He looks at me with disdain and talks to me like a man. He's barefoot and is riding bareback. The horse looks like him: in bad shape, his flanks sunken, missing fur in spots, his eyes empty. But the boy doesn't stick around, he takes off again at a frenetic gallop, probably to announce my arrival to the whole valley. I pass two hundred yards from the yurt where the boy's family must live. Custom demands that I stop, but I'm not going to. A woman comes out of the dwelling, an infant hanging from her breast. She has a gloomy expression, seeming to say, "What are *you* doing here?" I greet her and hurry on; she's indifferent. The dogs wake up and smell me on the wind. I'm still not used to these Mongolian mastiffs. They start to bark and become threatening; I need to hurry up. I walk along the stream to find a good place to get water, but there are too many yurts. This water must be full of laundry detergent residue, human and animal excrement, etc. I'll need to stop right away to avoid having all this bacteria and fifteen families' worth of germs proliferate in my water. I make a decision and quickly fill my water containers, promising myself that I'll treat this water with Micropur, then pass it through my water filter.

Suddenly, while I'm busy reattaching my water containers to my cart, an enormous dog approaches. I barely have time to protect myself using my cart as a shield. He plunges his fangs into the back of my cart with a certain passion, I must say. The attack lasts five minutes, which seems like an eternity. During this time, a bare-chested Mongolian observes the scene, caresses his belly, and leaves. He is apparently just waking up from his nap. He lays a sleepy eye on the dog who's tearing my cart and makes a gesture that seems to say, "You woke me up for that?" then goes back into his yurt. I call him, and he doesn't respond. Looks like it will be between me and the dog. I push my cart against him in short jabs, which causes him to let go, then he immediately plants his fangs again. My poor cart seems to hold up against the coup de grâce to the giant truck tire inner tube I stuck to the back to protect it from rocks. So I decide to move forward with this curious load in the back. A very bad idea. The dog is joined by other mastiffs; soon I count five of them. It's bizarre, they all seem completely wound up. I'm going to finish as hamburger meat if I don't do something soon. When I reach the next yurt, a man comes to my aid but, as he approaches, the dogs turn on him and show their fangs. He gives in to cowardice and retreats to his yurt, as though nothing were happening. I can't believe my eyes. I'm not shocked by the dogs, but by the humans. Then from afar comes a galloping horseman trailed by a cloud of dust. He stops just two feet from my cart. The horse is black, with a magnificent shiny coat, and the man is garbed in traditional attire. He holds himself erect, and there's something very noble about him. Our eyes meet. His superb leather saddle bears splendid red Mongolian inscriptions and drawings. Without a word, he removes the dogs with the help of his horse, whose courage is apparently equal to his beauty. I thank him. His regard meets mine in silence. He waits a bit longer to be sure the dogs don't gang up again, then with a small movement of his head, he goes back into the steppe as quickly as he came. I stand there with my jaw on the ground. I watch the cloud of dust depart. It takes me a few seconds to react and to get as far from these people as quickly as possible. I push my pace to put distance between myself and the dogs, but my spirit is with the man on the black horse. Who is he? The only real Mongolian in these steppes? It's a total mystery. I love these encounters where words are useless and silence reigns.

That day, I put up my tent beneath an old bridge made of logs, sheltered from prying eyes, hidden like an animal, but so happy to have this protective arch over my head. I make myself some tea and savor the calm. There's no one nearby, and all around me the steppes stretch out to infinity. "A day that ends well," I say to myself, smiling. The situation could have turned into a nightmare. These dogs are used to protect livestock from wolves and thieves. They're beautiful but imposing, and they're neither trained nor domesticated. Their size and thick coats are adapted to the conditions, specifically to the winters here. I'll call them the lions of the steppes. Not to mention that I'm not vaccinated against rabies. I quickly forget the attack and let my spirit dream about the image of the mysterious horseman. I watch my steaming teapot purr, I stare as though hypnotized until the water escapes the spout in little spurts. My usual good spirits return, and in a gesture I've repeated so many times, I fill my cup with the precious liquid.

I thank my protector.

The atmosphere is heavy, strangely so, and catching my breath even when I'm stopped is becoming difficult. I'm beneath my umbrella, sweating, or rather, losing water. The thermometer has passed 105°F and the wind is nonexistent, not the tiniest hint of a breeze. I'm anxious and on edge. The previous night was again disrupted by intrusions. And now I find myself before a plain nine miles long covered in dry clay with no hope of finding any shade. The ground reflects the heat so intensely that it feels like I'm walking on a hot plate! I cheer myself on; I absolutely must cross this plain. Go, Sarah Marquis! Go, Sarah Marquis, go! In these difficult moments I like to differentiate myself from her, as though she weren't me, so I encourage her aloud. It gives me energy. Hearing my own voice seems strange. This crossing will be no walk in the park, I'll have to divide it first into fifteen-minute stretches, then a break, and continue with a break every ten minutes. I'm worn out physically. The lack of sleep has caught up with me, my legs tremble beneath the weight of my load before I even start walking. I won't let myself look at the ground, where the tips of my feet appear at regular intervals. I keep my eyes fixed on the faraway horizon, to the place where I'm going. I won't lower them.

Four hours later, completely drained, I'm on the opposite edge of this plain, next to a paved road. I look at it with astonishment, as I hadn't expected to see it. The lack of sleep due to the repeated visits of night horsemen combined with this weather has drained me, emptied me, as though I've been drugged. I even feel apprehensive about crossing this road, and yet there's not a car on the horizon, not a sound. I laugh and chide myself, "So, Sarah Marquis, now you're scared of paved roads?"

I let myself be amused by my reaction and lift my head. I notice a strange-looking shack on the other side of the road, with red pillars gnawed by the wind. It's just sitting there, on the summit of the butte. Intrigued, I go and see what's up. I approach from the side, pulling my cart which, like me, is clumsy and tired. A man is sitting under the awning. With slow, regular movements, he is straightening rusty nails. He lifts his head, pauses a few seconds without a word, stares at me unblinkingly, then with a smile that seems to split his face in two, he motions for me to climb up. He calls out to me in perfect English.

"Where are you from? Where's your bicycle?"

"I'm from Switzerland, I'm walking."

"You're crazy! You're Swiss? Well then," he continues in French, "we'll be able to talk, come on up!"

These words come out of his mouth so naturally that I let go of my cargo and join him. He immediately suggests that I rest, but that first of all I have a good meal. It turns out that this Mongolian has worked as a guide, in the company of tourists, all his life. Now he's trying to start a camp of yurts that he has to take down before winter and put back up in the spring, but he lacks funds. I have so many questions on the subject of Mongolian people. I'm especially impatient to ask him why the Mongolians I meet lift up their T-shirt as soon as they see me. And even more: Why do they urinate whenever they meet me?

It's the end of the afternoon of my second day there, while having a good cup of tea, that I ask him these questions. He's instantly overcome by a fit of laughter that brings tears to his eyes. Fatigue being a factor, I can't keep myself from laughing hysterically, too. Our peals of laughter alert the cook who arrives with a dish towel in hand. Of a jovial nature, she leaves with the giggles: chain reaction. My questions will go unanswered. I'll sleep day and night, only leaving my yurt to eat, I'm so exhausted. After three days of this treatment, I put on my shoes and leave for Kharkhorin.

It's always hard to leave after a stop. I leave this place full of tranquility just before noon. The cook has made me a sort of hard wheat cake for the occasion, which I wrap as preciously as I would a gold ingot. A few hours later, I've already forgotten the humans and found my rhythm. But it did me good to talk with a human being who understood what I was saying. Before I left, he warned me about the likely change in the weather. "It always happens after Naadam (independence day)," he told me.

That night, I move my camp several times. The wind changes direction and intensity. I absolutely must find a spot that provides adequate shelter. I go back up along the only rock formation, a series of weird mini peaks poking out of the ground. I don't want to be caught unprepared by the storm, so I moor my tent to the ground with anything I can find. Satisfied, I look at the darkening sky. I slip into my tent without really settling in, I want to be ready just in case. I wait to see what the sky is holding in its belly. It seems very full. Rain begins the festivities. I have no doubts about the strength of my tent, it's one of the most robust on the market. As a precaution, I've dug furrows around it to allow the water to drain off quickly, in case it falls in great quantity. But I have a bad feeling about this, I can tell that things are unusually animated outside. An opening of a couple inches is enough for me to understand: it's a nightmare! The worst thing possible, I think at that moment (although the future will prove me wrong). An opaque wall is moving in my direction, not more than ten yards away, and it's hail—a tent's worst enemy! I put my shoes back on quickly, I'm ready to evacuate if I have to! No sooner are my shoes on my feet than my cloth house seems to tighten at the base. I yank open the rain fly and, horrified, I find myself staring down a mudslide that's ripping out everything in its path. In a flash I'm full of adrenaline. I have to act fast. My tent is emitting sounds that I've never heard before: it's fighting. With all my strength, I throw my pack onto a nearby ledge. I can't believe it! I use every ounce of strength I have to pull out my cart before this monster swallows it up completely, and me with it. I fight, it won't take me easily. I throw myself on the ground so I can grab on to the earth, pulling with all my might on one of the handles of my cart. The power the mudslide wields is extraordinary. My feet scramble on the ground, slide, I seize the handle that's slipping from my grasp. It only lasts a few minutes, but it seems like an eternity. Then everything stops, the storm has passed just as suddenly as it started. A gentle, fine rain caresses my face, the monster has passed! I collect myself, letting my body relax and splay out on the ground. I'm spent, but I didn't let go of my cart, it's safe and sound. I give a victory shout! I've won this battle.

I yell, "Mongolia, you won't take me!"

I was able to save my pack and my cart. Everything happened so fast. I'm soaked and covered in a grey paste. I find my tent, half buried. It's nothing more than a heap of mud, the balls of ice the size of Ping-Pong balls have torn it, without leaving it a chance. It fought bravely. I extract it and try to see if I can save it, but there's nothing worth saving.

I get out my video camera and capture this moment of uncertainty: it's nine o'clock at night, I have no roof, I don't know where I'm going to sleep, I'm cold, and the adrenaline is gone from my veins.

I decide to do what I know how to do: walk to warm myself up and maybe during the night find a rock that will protect me from the wind. For the moment I just need to survive this night, I can figure out the rest tomorrow.

I take a step. The team is not all here, my tent is no longer, I'm soaked, and it won't be long until night blankets everything in darkness. Without stopping, I nose about, scrutinizing every little change in the terrain before me with the concentration of a cat before a mouse hole, when suddenly a nomad on horseback approaches. It's the first time I've been happy to see a nomad after nine p.m.! He motions for me to follow him; I respond with a simple nod of the head. We thread ourselves through the scenery, he on horseback and I pushing my cart. We soon arrive at a stream situated below us. He points to his yurt that stands on the other side, on the opposite bank. I realize there was one important activity that was missing from today's schedule: swimming! I smile. To think that just two hours ago I'd thought that it was the end of my day!

The stream is overflowing and continues to swell before our eyes. I put my pack on the horseman's back, which he doesn't like one bit, and yet he makes a first crossing and puts my pack on the dry bank. The water is so high that his horse has to swim. He comes back for my cart, then for me. But this last crossing on horseback is suddenly too dangerous: the water level has continued to rise and the current has become violent. The nomad refuses to take the risk, which I understand. The only thing left to do is swim. And I'd better do it quickly. I walk three hundred yards upstream. I think it's far enough. I calculate my likely trajectory: with the force of the current, I should arrive just in front of their camp. Just as I'm about to jump in the water, I hear whistles from the other bank. A smiling young man on horseback launches himself into the tumultuous water. The animal swims with difficulty, his head held out of the water, his nostrils flared. Still smiling, his rider has made it to my bank and is positioning his horse for the return trip. Without a word, I move toward him, he grabs my forearm and I grab his, and he propels me with incredible force onto the back of his horse. He tells me to hold onto his waist, as I'm sitting on the horse's hindquarters. And now this poor horse has to fight against the current this time with two passengers. We make it to the opposite bank, beneath the excited gaze of children who run to meet us, the barking of dogs who welcome us, and the smile of the head of the family. I thank everyone, including the horse. The little group then hurries toward the yurt, with me bringing up the rear. Smiling, I think to myself, "At least I avoided an icy bath." Mud has also flowed here; the bottom of the yurt is covered with a thick layer of it, and a woman with long black hair moves back and forth with a metal bucket and a large cloth in the guise of a mop. She's skinny, frail, her hair sticks to her sweaty face. No one helps her. I stand up to greet her and give her a hand, but the little girls vigorously hold me back. All these men and all these children of the family will let her break her back all alone for over an hour cleaning the yurt's floor. I feel sorry for her. The four inches of mud on the ground wouldn't have been a match for a good broom, but the woman has nothing to work with but a rag.

Much later, this scene was explained to me as follows: women are responsible for all that happens inside the yurt, and men for everything concerning the exterior. Each never interferes with the work of the other.

The ten- and twelve-year-old girls play the role of hostess and ask me lots of questions, making it an event. I get out my little dictionary and everyone settles in next to the entryway, sitting on sawed-off stumps. Mud is everywhere around us, and the daylight is fading. The moment before the night becomes all black, the woman sticks her head out of the yurt's only opening and gives us the order to come back in. She's made a fire, and on the small central stove is a large dish giving off steam and the smell of warm milk. The woman asks the girls to go get something for her. Then she bends down on the ground to break up a brick of tea. She has a worn stone in her right hand and crushes the whole thing with a regular, practiced movement as she lifts the bit of cloth containing the tea. To my great surprise, the young man who came to get me on his horse is not a family member; like me, he is sitting on the guests' side. I'm cold, I'm exhausted, and I'm wet. The girls come back with buckets full of dried animal dung and hurry to build up the fire. As soon as they're done, they glue themselves to me. The little one is on my lap, while the big one lays her head on my shoulder. It works for me, as it shifts the young man who took me on his horse two places down the line. I'm not used to such immediate intimacy with another person. Communal life is so far from my solitary existence.

The tea is ready. It's served in a bowl, and the next in line must wait for the first to finish before he passes it along. In this way, all the refugees of this tumultuous night enjoy the right to a bowl of hot tea. Throughout the exercise, I detect not a trace of impatience from those present. The bowl is filled many times with this liquid that will so pleasantly radiate heat through its recipients. The warm steam that escapes from the basin on the stove also heats the inside of the yurt, and it gradually warms up. I can't stay awake any longer, my eyes are closing on their own even as I fight it. I decide to thank the mistress of the house and I sign to her that I'll sleep with an empty stomach, as I can't keep my eyes open. Without waiting for her to answer, I quickly roll out my mattress far to the left, toward the door. I know that they won't get up before nine o'clock the next morning and I'll have left well before then. I slip into my sleeping bag completely dressed, with sharp looks from everyone. I turn my back on them and try to fall asleep. I hear the mistress of the house juggle her pots; she's going to feed eight people with boiled mutton. The whole group will go to bed around midnight, with full bellies. When all the noises have stopped, I finally fall into a deep sleep. Suddenly, an arm moves across the sleeping bag and holds me tight. I jump and turn over faster than a burning crêpe—it's my neighbor who's snuggled up next to me. I push him away violently but in silence. Five minutes after the first incident, he tries again, but this time my eyes are wide open. In his language, I instruct him to stop. A few minutes later my eyes are closing again when a croaking sound makes me jump. An enormous toad has decided to pay me a visit. He's right next to my head, and he looks at me without moving. He's taken advantage of the bottom edge of the yurt's being tied up off the ground—so the floor can dry—to inspect the place. Under the influence of exhaustion, I get a bad case of the giggles, which I stifle by hiding inside my sleeping bag so as not to wake anyone up.

To sum up: if I turn to my right, I find a young Mongolian who almost certainly has an erection, and if I turn to my left, I find a prehistoric-looking toad as big as my hand. Just then, a wandering hand climbs up my spine. Time to act! Without turning around, I swing a blind fist with all my might in my neighbor's direction. I don't know where I get him, but the sounds of pain at my blow confirm that I hit my target. I continue to look at my toad, who's looking better all the time, despite his slimy appearance. Without any hesitation, my choice is made: it'll be the toad.

Despite all this, I am truly happy to spend the night somewhere dry, beneath a roof. I let myself glide into a sleep that's been calling me for hours. My last thoughts are, *Thank you, I'm sleeping under a roof.*

I've finally closed my eyes, like all the others, when suddenly the door bangs open. The mistress of the house jumps and turns on a flashlight. Two fat Mongolians in spiffy city clothes have planted themselves in front of the fire, yelling, as is their habit, without taking into account the hour and without any consideration for the people who are sleeping. The woman sits down, stokes the fire, and makes them some food. My eyes are open again, my ears strain toward the fire. I hear them recounting their adventures. I understand that they're stranded because they couldn't cross the bridge upstream. "There's water everywhere," exclaims the smaller of the two. The husband gets up and joins the little group around the fire.

Until dawn, they make merry, laugh, eat. It's not until the

first glow of daylight that everyone goes to bed. I bid good morning to my toad who hasn't moved and I turn around. To my great surprise, my neighbor isn't there. Just then I hear a horse leaving at a gallop behind the yurt. Maybe he has a black eye. I make my way out of the yurt as quietly as possible and find my cart outside, where I left it, beneath my tarp. I search for the sewing kit that I'd brought with me for just such an occasion. During this time, one of the dogs comes to greet me, and I stop to stroke him. The door of the yurt opens and the woman appears: "What are you doing outside so early? Come inside quick where it's warm, I'll make you some tea!"

I politely refuse with a smile, thank her for her hospitality with the rudimentary Mongolian I've acquired so far, then motion for her to go back inside and sleep a little. She returns my smile. I give her the sewing kit with a rubber band and a few of my bandages. She thanks me, bowing her head several times. Looking at her now, she's another woman, radiant despite the lack of sleep. She puts my wet pack on my back and accompanies me for the first hundred yards. Then she lets me go.

I go north; I have to cross the paved road in a few miles, according to my estimates. Here everything is flooded and I need a tent in order to continue. While walking, I weigh the pros and cons, and I finally decide to head back toward the camp of my French-speaking friend. From there, I can call my contact in Ulaanbaatar so he can send me a new tent.

I approach the camp at the end of the day. Debris is flying everywhere, it's been devastated. The yurts situated on the butte escaped the flood, but the previous night's storm got the better of the three others. The proprietor is on the roof of a yurt, trying to stabilize the whole thing with some straps. I put down my things and run to give him a hand. The wind has kicked up again, which makes each maneuver delicate. Once the last yurt is reinforced with the help of the straps, he invites me inside and offers me some tea. He tells me about the storm, the lightning, and the hail. "The entire region's been flooded, you can't go anywhere. Cars can't get through from the other side, the road is closed," he explains. He's quiet and sad. So I tell him about my adventure, the crossing on horseback, my choice between the toad and the young man. He immediately starts laughing so hard that it makes him forget his bad luck. Then he adds, "Welcome to Mongolia!"

I stay with him for three days waiting for my temporary replacement tent. The weather is not good, there will be more rain, more storms. He suggests another route where he knows there are never floods: travel due west to a mini pass, and from there progress toward the south. After a few miles, I'll meet up with a new trail that should take me to Kharkhorin. Looking at my maps, he explains how far the flood has reached and offers to drop me off at the pass. Up there, I'll be out of harm's way, but I'll have to wait for the water to recede a little so that his car, a lifted four-wheel drive vehicle, can pass. After scrutinizing my maps, I conclude that it's my only option. I don't want to be stuck here for three months! The new route is thirty miles longer, but at least I'll be able to get out of here. In the meantime, my Mongolian contact hasn't found a single mode of transport going in my direction. . . . "People aren't crazy, no one wants to go where there's flooding!" But he took the initiative of sending one of his guys by car to personally drop off a replacement tent that he normally uses for the tours he organizes. Things are coming together beautifully.

Two days later, early in the morning, my Mongolian friend asks me for money in order to fill up the car he's going to use to take me up to the pass. He has to travel east, to a tiny town, then once the gas tank is full, come back. Only then will departure be possible.

In the early afternoon of the same day, we arrive, after a journey full of pitfalls, at the pass in question, which according to my GPS is located forty-eight miles west of the camp. He drops me off without stopping the motor and takes off immediately, out of fear that the water will rise again, which would leave him stranded on the wrong side of the river. As he drives away, he waves at me through his open window. I watch the vehicle disappear slowly, absorbed by the line on the horizon. All around me, the flat steppe unfolds for miles and miles. The floods are behind me.

I'm going to throw myself into this open plain, as one throws oneself into the sea on a life raft. There's no apparent shelter— not a rock, not a tree, not a village—for a few hundred miles.

Days and nights succeed one another until I lose count. Only the moon keeps me informed of what I need to know and nothing more. What use is it to me to know that it's Tuesday? This wind that never sleeps devours me like a worm from the inside. The wind is so violent that I spend my nights clinging to the central tent poles just to keep my tent on the ground. At any moment we could be carried away. The lack of sleep starts to weigh on me, to wear on my body and even more on my spirit. I struggle, I rage, I meditate, I fight with all my strength. I fight hour after hour, dreaming that the daylight will deliver me from my ordeal.

Yet it's all these events taken together that will connect me with invisible and unbreakable lines to this land. Horses are part of my daily life. I often wake up to the sound of their unbridled galloping around my tent, sometimes they follow me for miles and amuse themselves with me. In certain moments, I feel like I'm part of their herd, that they've accepted me. I imagine galloping without limits in the open steppe, with neither pack nor cart. I would feel the wind in my mane. Yup, that's what my dreams are made of.

I admire these beasts, they're majestic. I've spent so much time with them, observing them. (Have people who eat horse meat ever looked a horse in the eyes?) And yet, alone before this space, facing this wind that seems to want to eat my nerves, I'm weakening. As if these extreme conditions weren't enough, another storm imposes itself.

On this day, I'm happy to stop walking, to find myself in my tent, and to stop fighting. I put up my tent directly facing the wind, even if I know perfectly well that it will change direction three more times, the last time right around nine p.m. My cloth house is not protected, not a rock, not a depression in the ground. I will have to endure this wind another night.

I'm sitting cross-legged in front of my tent, tea is boiling at my feet. I've finally taken off my shoes. Suddenly I jump, a horseman is coming at full throttle, galloping in from behind the right side of my tent. His horse has a caramel coat, a lively regard, such a presence that I surprise myself when I flash him a smile. My eyes leave the horse to examine the horseman. The rider is a young man clothed in a shabby coat of a dubious brown. I can barely make out the woven inserts composed of eight traditional diamond shapes. His cloth waist belt is bright orange, he's wearing traditional tall leather boots and a cap faded by the sun. He sits down without saying hello, as is the custom here, and watches me cook. Silently, he moves closer to me, examining the details of my face and does not seem to like what he sees. He backs off a bit, with an expression of disdain, as though he's eaten something bad. I'm tired, and I'm sick of being observed like a monkey. Suddenly, I have an idea. I pick up my camera and I take his picture. He jumps backward, and "Alley-oop, I'm back on my horse" and "Alley-oop, I'm galloping away into the steppe." Very soon he's nothing more than a speck on the horizon. I giggle. I've just discovered a secret weapon that will change my life in the steppe.

All of a sudden, I see my cooking pot take off rolling into the steppe with the garlicky buckwheat that I've just finished cooking still in it. The wind gust is violent. I turn around and hear myself utter, "Oh, my God!" A red wall of sand is advancing on me. The last time I saw anything like it was in a movie.

There's nowhere to take shelter, there isn't a rock I can hold on to, nothing. I feel powerless. Before this thing arrives on top of me, I absolutely have to remove my tent poles. I only have time to unhook them without pulling them out. I lie down, placing my whole body over my tent for fear that all my gear will fly away into the steppe and be lost forever. The rain precedes the sand. I'm barefoot, wearing a T-shirt, my Gore-Tex jacket is in my pack, inside my tent, inaccessible. I hope that my weight will be enough to keep everything on the ground. The rain is now so hard that it stings my skin like tiny nails, but it's the least of my worries. The ground trembles. That's my real concern. Lightning falls all around me, just a few yards away. Blue lines plunge from the sky at an amazingly sustained rhythm. I'm freezing cold; I let my head sink between my hands and breathe calmly. I think, *It will pass, everything passes, and this storm will, too.* I stop looking; I wait. The ground continues to tremble, lightning strikes not far away. And then, like a well-orchestrated third act, the sandstorm comes pelting down on me. I clench my jaw a little longer, I know it will soon be over. Then nothing. I get up slowly, the air is cool, clear of all tension. I raise my head toward the sky: "Really? That's all you've got in store? That's it?"

Everything is calm. The sand is mixed with the water and I'm drenched to the bone. I immediately notice that my stove flew off with my pot. It's the post-apocalypse: the sky allows beams of light to appear through huge formations of black clouds. I stand up and realize that I survived, by pure chance. An overwhelming emotion of gratitude washes over me. *Thank you, thank you . . .*

Suddenly, a muffled rumble of thunder causes me to lift my head. Like a wild beast I sniff the open plain with all my senses. I conclude that the wind has turned. Is the storm coming back? Yes, it's coming back. "OK, move." I say to myself aloud. Hearing my voice gives me energy.

With gestures repeated countless times, I stuff everything into my cart, and get out my Gore-Tex gear that I zip at breakneck speed over my wet clothes. Once everything is folded up, I decide to go on a quest for my indispensable stove and my sole cooking pot. I shout for joy: five hundred yards from camp they're stuck beneath one of the rare bushes of the steppe. I assess: nothing broken, nothing lost.

At this exact moment, the rain starts again. I realize that night has fallen abruptly—at least, that's what it seems like. Equipped with a headlamp, I start moving quickly along the path to look for a potential shelter. I push my cart with all my might and my body slowly warms up thanks to the sustained rhythm I inflict on it. The thunder gets closer. My thoughts tumble through my head. I won't be able to put up my tent tonight, so I'll have to walk, let the storm pass, continue until dawn if I have to; but I'm going to have to stop if the lightning starts back up!

After barely an hour, a yurt appears in the beam of my headlamp, with lots of little glowing eyes all around it. I immediately head toward it. When I'm twenty yards away, I call out in the night to inform the nomad who lives there of my presence. A dog I can't see barks madly; I imagine it ready to attack. The sheep surrounding the yurt seem to respond to the dog's barking in a cacophony of baaing. They're agitated, terrified by the storm. A silhouette appears suddenly, studies me. I can't see the face. The person yells at the dog to hush, which it does, to my astonishment. It's the silhouette of a woman. She approaches. She's not calm, I can sense her nervousness. She stops a reasonable distance away, and I mime what happened to me. After a long moment of reflection, she motions for me to come inside. I thank her so many times that she sticks a cup of tea under my nose to make me stop. I'm safe here, I can feel it. *Thank you, thank you . . .*

Three children are sleeping. Looking around, I discover a new universe. Horses' halters are carefully organized, everything is very clean. Leather straps, ready to be worked, are also suspended at regular intervals along the circular structure of wooden beams that hold up the yurt. The mistress of the house is wearing a traditional coat-dress that falls to her feet, night blue and embellished with images sewn in black thread. She is beautiful, thin, and her features indicate that she doesn't come from here but almost certainly from the mountains to the west, at the border of Kazakhstan. Her skin, bronzed by the sun, is smooth in places and folded in others. In the intimacy of the light thrown by the small stove's flames, she explains life here. During the storm, the animals become frightened and get hopelessly lost or struck by lightning if there's no one there to guide them. It's therefore imperative to be with them and to sing them the song about the sun and the blue sky. "It calms the animals and reassures them." I'm in the home of real nomads! What incredible luck.

She confirms what I had supposed: her husband is at that moment with the herd. Then she sits awhile in silence before speaking again. She's clearly worried.

Much later, I'll learn that there are lots of accidents during these summer storms and that many husbands, men, and adolescents don't come back after their nocturnal adventures. She goes outside every so often and looks at the night, and I go with her. Outside, lightning is the key player on this summer night. The woman inhales the darkness as though communicating with her husband, as though she can smell him, sense him, without a word. Yet her tense face expresses no emotion. Suddenly, she gestures for me to come inside. I glance at the nighttime spectacle, flashes of lightning overlap so regularly that it's no longer possible to count them.

Inside, we hear almost nothing, everything is peaceful. The children are still sleeping.

I can only salute the magnificent construction that is the cylindrical tent. Once again, it fascinates me, but this time with its solidity.

During the night, I drift in and out of sleep. The woman will remain at her nighttime post by the fire. The stove illuminates her tense features. At dawn, an exhausted man comes through the door. There's no kiss, no gesture, nothing but an exchange of looks, but the essential is there in their silence. After a few swallows of tea, I guess that the woman is explaining the reason for my presence. He glances at me, and I take the opportunity to greet him with a nod. He signals his acceptance of my company while eating and I join him next to the fire. On the menu: rice and milk. The only dish I can eat (meat-free)! I smile and devour my bowl, to the obvious pleasure of the woman.

Daylight has returned and I say my good-byes to this beautiful family. My cart and I forge a path through the sheep resting around the yurt, the air is clear and fresh. I turn around. The family is watching me leave, they are all smiling. Words are useless. *Thank you, thank you* . . . you are the true nomads!

My legs find their rhythm, the steppe stretches before me as far as I can see, the morning light caresses the countryside. The following days will have the usual end-of-day storm. And yet, from here on, things are different. Every evening, starting at four o'clock, I study the horizon, full of hope, searching for a livestock shelter. They've appeared in the creases of the countryside, to my great happiness. They're just a few boards clumsily assembled for the winter and yet, for me, they're a real shelter that protects me from the ferocity of the storms.

And then one day, the little city of Kharkhorin materializes on the horizon, nestled at the foot of the mountains. After my joy at having found it, I feel apprehension at finding myself once again with my companions, humans. I know that it will be another dusty little hole, and that it will be difficult to find food. I'm so hungry that I don't have a choice, I have to use Kharkhorin as a resupply stop. For days I've rationed myself to a bowl of rice per day. I divide it in two. In the morning, I mix my white rice with powdered coffee and at night, with a pinch of salt. It occurs to me that my arrivals in town are practically choreographed. I will have to eat, shower, sleep, buy food, and leave. Nothing exceptional in these basic needs. Except that, beneath the Mongolian sky, each step of this process is a real challenge. A bit like an adventure within an adventure.

I'm always careful to arrive in town well before nightfall. After getting my bearings, I finally discover a camp for tourists on the outskirts of the city where I'll be able to sleep.

I put my belongings in a small yurt with a bright orange interior. Collapsing heavily on my bed, I lie there, eyes closed, not moving, for a few moments. After a long moment, I open my eyes. Usually being in constant motion, it feels good to be still, knowing I have a roof over my head. How I love to lie down and contemplate this ceiling constructed from thick, painted wooden sticks, connected at the summit by a solid ring of wood functioning both as a skylight and as structural reinforcement.

You find this circular mode of habitation—portable, no less—all the way up to the high Himalayan plateau. I've even seen them in Buryatia, in the taiga to the south of Siberia.

The fire is the central activity of the yurt, which seems obvious to me. In my sedentary life, when I'm not walking, I often end the day with a fire. The serenity that the flames give me is beyond words. They seem to comfort me, give me energy, but more than anything, they possess the gift of suspending time.

Here, wood was long ago replaced by dried animal dung. The first time I saw a woman, a basket on her back and a strange little curved stick in her hand, striding zigzag across the steppe, I wondered what she could possibly be gathering. She was blindly flicking something from the ground into the basket behind her. I stayed several long minutes, watching her through my binoculars, wondering what could be the content of her find . . . until she missed her target, and I saw a nice, big turd go flying through the air! Even today I still laugh about that candid little scene. I loved learning about the life of the nomads this way. Watching them, trying to interpret their gestures, discovering new clues each day.

In my yurt, I squat next to the stove. I insert several pieces of dried dung and light the fire as one would expect, with the gas lighter provided, exactly the same model that we use in our kitchens at home. . . .

I enter a building that is similar to a chicken house at home. Brick buildings here defy natural law; nothing is straight, nothing is level.

But if I think about it, the children here don't entertain themselves with Legos, they play with vertebrae from the backbones of sheep. . . . So it makes sense, I think.

The nomads seem blank, with no mental formatting. This can have great advantages, as I will discover throughout this year spent at their side.

The shower wall is grey and unfinished. There's only a trickle of boiling water flowing from it. I can't do anything with it, except burn myself. I go back to my yurt to get my titanium cooking pot to use as a mixing faucet. Completely naked, I collect a little hot water and add some of the icy water flowing from another faucet near the ground. Crouched down, I try to wash myself as well as I can. It's been weeks since I've been able to wash; I've been dreaming of it. Normally, it takes several showers to remove all the built-up layers of sweat. But I already feel relatively clean. I've succeeded at washing my hair, which is nice, since I'll be able to stop scratching my scalp. I'd really started to look flea-ridden and my hair was starting to transform into dreadlocks. The water seems to have generously erased all of my hiker's woes. Beneath all these layers of sweat, I finally uncover the woman that I am. Feeling the water run over my body is my way of wiping away the memory of these past weeks that have been so difficult, even agonizing.

I fill one last pot of boiling water that I bring back to my yurt. In it I delicately place the precious eggs I bought from an old lady in the street. I figure that they won't take long to cook.

I won't open my eyes again until the next afternoon. . . . I've slept twenty-four hours in a row, I was exhausted. My body took what it needed: hours of sleep—and my eggs are cooked!

I have to allow myself more than two complete days of sleep before I leave again.

Steppe, you will not take me. . . .

After laying eyes on human faces, I decide to leave toward the southwest as planned, following a dirt road. Days pass, the

steppe changes colors. In moments it makes me think of a mul-
tilayered cake. It's neither a raspberry nor lemon color, but more
of a warm amber placed on top of all of the possible greens as-
sociated with the sky blue of this place: so open and unchang-
ing. The whole thing is almost beautiful. But unfortunately it
doesn't last. The huge, end-of-day storms often ruin this almost-
perfect painting in seconds.

I once again lose any notion of what day it is, to my great
happiness. An occasional telephone call to Switzerland recon-
nects me to reality. Yesterday I talked to my dog, as I always do
while I'm out on expedition. As soon as the telephone rings at
my parents' house, D'Joe looks at my mother and cocks his head,
as if to say, "Is it her?" My mom has always played this game
with him. And once our human discussion has ended, she says,
"Here's D'Joe, OK?"

In Switzerland, everyone's doing well. I'm glad. On that side
of the planet, they follow me thanks to my tracker, which indicates my exact position at any moment, reassuring them.

It's been more than a week now since I left Kharkhorin. I wake
up, I've slept almost an entire night. Outside it's daytime, and
yet, in my tent, it's dark. . . . Yesterday at the end of the day, I
spotted a great big drainpipe. I slipped under the dirt road, and
taking care that no one saw me, I quickly crawled inside, followed by my pack and my cart. Then I waited, waited for something to happen, for someone to appear, as usual. Two hours
later, no one had come, except a big black dog that came to mark
his territory, barely missing my gear. I was happy to see the dog,
and gave him one of my precious cookies. I so miss my sweet

D'Joe. During the night, I felt the base of my tent being tugged and jerked. I opened the zipper. In the shadows I could make out the silhouette of my friend the dog who had come back for more cookies. I scolded him gently. He leaned his body into mine and gave me a few licks on the face. He seemed to say, "You're not mad, are you?" I couldn't stop myself from giving him a big hug, despite the fleas and other creepy-crawlies doubtless hiding in his thick coat. All this without turning on my flashlight, for fear of being seen. And naturally I shared my ration of biscuits with him. This morning, I realize that these concrete drainpipes might offer a real long-term solution for my safety. I decide that instead of heading due south, I'm going to follow this path, even if it goes a little too far west for my taste. I'm hoping that this way I'll be able to sleep without being disturbed. For a certain period, nights are a joy, I'm finally able to rest and sleep deeply. These cold, windy culverts are palaces for me. From this point on, my days of walking no longer end in terror.

Mongolia is like a truly beautiful person. From up close, you can't quite determine if the eyes are beautiful, or if the mouth is exceptional, but with a bit of distance you perceive a harmonious blend with an indescribable energy.

This is Mongolia. Its beauty breathes. It's the space, the absence of limits, the absence of everything—roads, fences, rules. The farther away you move, the more you see it. I'm completely hypnotized by the beauty of these steppes. Which surprises even me.

———

I haven't seen anyone in days. I avoid the nomads. I gather water below the road, and find enough. It's a little sad to spend my days in the great outdoors and find myself squatting, living like a sewer rat at nightfall. Often, I'm forced to share space with the decomposing bodies of animals: poor beasts who were looking for refuge to hide and die with dignity. Their carcasses give off putrid odors.

But my spirit is elsewhere; my priority is simply to live in safety. So I will follow this strip of earth without deviating, day after day, with the assurance of a night without drama at the end of each day of walking.

I arrive with apprehension at the gates of Khujirt, wary of encountering humans again. As soon as I get there, I set about providing for the essential: food. I succeed in finding rice, onions, garlic, oil, and *bolzaks* (the famous, traditional hard cookies). This will be my food for the next fifteen days. The nomads fix me with hard stares. The children hide from my glances behind their mothers' long coats, then spy on me with one uncertain eye. I walk without worrying about people. I've stopped saying hello. I do as they do, I ignore just about every rule of manners. I pause in front of a yurt that seems to be a restaurant. I'm dirty, yet I approach, curious to see what people have in their bowls. I go stand in line like everyone else. When it's my turn, the woman supervising the two huge, steaming pots of boiled mutton gives me a blank stare. I ask her for rice and an egg. Without replying, she cooks me an egg over easy in a pool of mutton grease. I smile at her, pay, and go outside to find a place to squat on the ground. I'm so happy to have an egg; they're so rare, and it's my only source of protein.

People are scattered around the yurt, sitting in the grass with their noses in their bowls. No one speaks to anyone. Do they know each other, or is this just a rest stop along the way? Some horses are tied, others take advantage of the lull to graze a little around the yurt. I don't look at anyone and no one looks at me. While eating, I realize that each and every one of us has one thing in common: we are all very hungry. The faces before me are weather-beaten, the people in traditional garb, slim and athletic. The fat Mongols have disappeared from the country-side. I finish my bowl quickly, I'm so hungry. I go back in to see the cook for another bowl, but this time, the woman sends me away like a mangy dog, yelling and gesticulating at me. People lift their noses from their bowls, look at me severely, and shake their heads. I exit quickly without really knowing what could have provoked such animosity.

I wait around a little longer until the people leave. There are just a few nomads left slurping their bowls when a man urinates one meter to my left, splashing my cart a little. I look at him, and he acts as though nothing is happening. I can't stop myself from saying, "Your little willy just peed on my cart, sir!"

Pensive, I begin to analyze the situations I've found myself in, the men I've come across here and the way they act toward me. It doesn't have much to do with their past, but it has every-thing to do with a surplus of testosterone. They act like a pack of dogs. Next time I'll say, "What can I do for you, Fido?" I smile to myself . . . and realize that these Mongolians are starting to get on my nerves. That's it, I decide that I won't leave without a second bowl of rice. Once again, I infiltrate the yurt cafeteria. I nod my head and make a sound like a grunt (as I've seen done so many times) to the woman in charge of the operation. I assume that she's the boss; she has a ladle in her hand and doesn't seem to want to put it down. She glances toward the back, grumbles, and discretely smiles at me as she slides a bowl of egg perched on rice that she's already prepared for me. From behind the pots she checks that no one is watching, takes my money, and motions for me to leave quickly. I thank her profusely and slip outside to the sound of the stifled laughter of the woman and her accomplices. Once outdoors, I fill my poor stomach that hadn't dared hope for anything more.

She must have violated who knows what code to feed me. *Thank you, thank you . . .*

During these three years of walking, in each country I will cross, independent of their language, their culture, or their social status, women will find a way to fill my walker's stomach. But not only this; through their generosity, they will be sources of energy who also feed my heart. It is this that will allow me to hang on and take one step more. Hunger doesn't need translation, hunger expresses itself in universal language. On this day, in central Mongolia, this woman gives me a marvelous gift: she reminds me that I am part of the planet's tribe of women. And that between them, women must help each other and not tear each other down. I draw away, my belly full, my heart breathing deeply. . . . *Thank you, thank you . . .*

4. Gobi Desert

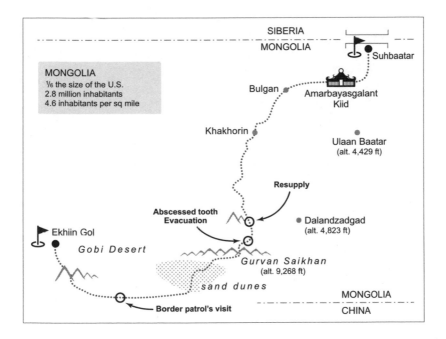

GUSTS OF WIND LIFT EVERYTHING IN THEIR PATH. THE ground has a caramel color that I love. Despite my isolated position, I can make out an electric line that appears to be running south. Looking at the horizon, I feel for my compass that's attached to a red string, which is attached to the zipper of my right pants pocket. The compass reading confirms the possibility of following the electric poles; they will guide me to my next destination, almost one hundred miles away. And once night falls, an electric pole will be a good mooring to which I can tie my tent. I haven't been finding livestock shelters or roads equipped with culverts recently.

I start a crossing that will play out between the sand, the wind, and me. I've found it—pure delight—nearly one hundred miles without humans, finally! It's steeped in familiar gestures, with the rhythm of my legs, who seem to understand the scope of the challenge.

Full of the peace and energy of the desert, I enter a hamlet. It's like all the other little villages I've seen: devoid of charm, empty, equipped with a dusty main street. As soon as I arrive, I start the hunt for the local market, but nothing is indicated; there are no signs, as usual. I spot some cars in front of a building. I put down my equipment there, go through the first door and then the second. I find myself in a small, dark room with a counter blocking access to the merchandise. A veil of smoke perfumes the windowless room. A shirtless, smooth-chested man is lying belly up on some bags of rice. His skin is waxy, a mixture of bad sweat and the mucous of old dreams washed up without further hope on his flabby paunch. His eyes are bloodshot and he pulls on his joint slowly and with obvious enjoyment.

A woman is behind the counter, but doesn't turn around when I enter. I call out to her, she doesn't respond. I've already been waiting for twenty minutes, and I'm the only customer. Clearly, this woman doesn't know how determined I am. With nearly every encounter, I experience this disdain for foreigners accompanied by a bit of a power play. I've grown used to it. However, I'm not going to leave here without a pack full of food. Suddenly, a man wearing city clothes and an honest face comes through the door and politely greets me. He gives his shopping list to the grocer who jumps to action, her eyes riveted to the piece of paper. I take the opportunity to start up a conversation with the visitor. He tells me about a place a short ways away where a woman puts up people passing through in her yurt. I also ask him why the grocer is ignoring me. Just at that moment she turns around, bearing on the left side of her face a blue-black mark, yellow around the edge.

"Are you saying," he asks, "that she won't serve you?"

He becomes angry, turns to face her, and flings words at her that seem to wound more than the blow she sports on her cheek. The tone rises, as it will in Mongolian conversations: tirades ricochet across the room and seem to bounce off the shop's floor and back at the woman. I don't understand what's happening, but I'm guessing she's being put in her place. The atmosphere is heavy and tense. The woman looks at me with an invitation to duel glowing in the depths of her eyes. She has "bad attitude" written all over her, and I step back a bit to avoid a potential projectile. God knows what she has at hand behind the counter. She serves me without a word, charges me a third more than the normal price, but I say nothing. I just want to be able to eat. I put the money on the counter and hurry to get out of there. A few minutes later, I arrive at the town's only fuel pump. A teenager sits on the skeleton of a rusty chair, while his friend steps up to meet me, a girl his age at his heels. He fills my one-liter bottle, I give him exact change. The seated boy stands up and lets fly with a surprise fist to the kidney of the young man who served me, for no apparent reason. The other spins around and retaliates violently with a punch to the face; the first one hits back. I yell, "That's enough!" Both of their faces are covered with blood. The two teenagers suspend their movement and look at me, astonished. But the more vicious of the two takes advantage of the downtime to hit his buddy with a good right jab.

I'm getting the feeling this place has a dark side. I fly out of there as fast as I can. I walk along the high wooden barricades that surround each yurt and finally arrive at the home of the woman who'll be able to host me for the night. The man I met

85

at the market has already come by to let her know I might be coming. She's waiting impatiently for me and brings me into the courtyard. We pass in front of an open door; I see a woman squatting on the ground cutting meat with a cleaver. She looks up and smiles at me, showing with no shyness her two remaining teeth. I greet her, returning her generous smile—smiles are so rare here! My yurt is at the back of the courtyard, next to a big, black dog attached to a two-foot chain. He practically strangles himself each time he moves, poor thing.

I'm happy, despite everything, to have a roof over my head. I go inside, take off my shoes, and collapse on the mattress. A few minutes later, two men burst into my yurt at full throttle as if they are a commando unit unto themselves responding to the call of duty! They're dressed in black city clothes. I observe them. They're here for something specific, they're clearly not the police. The news of the arrival of a stranger must have traveled through the village quickly. I let them look at my things and nose around. After a few minutes, I gesture that I want to sleep and push them gently toward the exit. The skinnier of the two has fire in his eyes that he fixes on me. I keep calm, showing no emotion whatsoever and start yawning to emphasize my indifference. But suddenly I've had enough, it's been a long day, I'm tired, and I'm sick of this village full of crazy people. I raise my voice and shout, "Get out of here!" To my great surprise and my even greater joy, they leave. And they don't return.

Little time passes before the old lady comes to see me, sitting down right next to me. She has the mischievous eyes of an experienced bargainer that tell me she's not exactly a stranger to the commandos' visit.

"Are you hungry?" she asks.

I take out my book of images and show her the rice and eggs. Two hours later, she wakes me holding a small dish of cold rice and two cold eggs over easy. It takes me less than a minute to eat all of it, I'm so hungry. I make some tea that we drink together in front of the yurt, while horrible shrieks emanate from behind the tall wooden fence. Every hair on my body stands on end, and a moment later, projectiles land in the courtyard, just missing us. The dog seems used to it and doesn't move. I glance through the gaps between the planks of wood and see a thin man who's screaming, barefoot, and wearing pants that are nothing but a piece of patched cloth. He walks with difficulty, shaking his head mechanically, and he seems to be paralyzed on one side. The danger passed, I'm sad. I feel sorry for this poor young man. I turn toward the woman who continues to calmly drink her tea. I plead the dog's case, with his too-short chain. Suddenly, she gets up and illustrates the happiness in which this big ball of fur luxuriates by giving him a disingenuous pat with the tips of her fingers that surprises even the dog!

You're a clever one, I think, *I'm going to have to keep my eye on you.* She's full of mischief. Still, I can't help but smile, there's something touching about her. I look at her anew, and I think it's her deep wrinkles that move me. One thing is strange, though: she allows me to discreetly observe her face in greater detail. It gives me the strange impression of walking through the door that leads to her private life, her story.

I turn my gaze away and swallow another sip of tea, when the wise words of an Aborigine whom I met years ago echo in a gentle voice deep within me: you don't steal a person's story, a plant's story, a tree's story, you wait patiently until they deign to share it with you.

At that moment, she lifts her head to smile at me, but this time her face is soft, her smile profound and honest. She just smiled at me with her soul.

The sun is setting. I go out in the night to see the moon. It's full and so beautiful that it keeps me from sleeping, as it sometimes will. In back, the proprietress is trying to close the fence's large gate. I help her, she smiles. Meanwhile, a pack of dogs comes by to taunt the poor, chained beast. I beg the woman with gestures to let him run and play with his friends. To my astonishment, she unhooks him and he goes to join the pack, trotting lightly. To my even greater surprise, at dawn he's back again, waiting in front of the gate to become a voluntary prisoner.

You won't catch me doing that! At the first light of day, I slip quietly out of this miserable place. I'm prepared: I have water, basic food, and fuel for my stove. I don't need anything other than my precious freedom. My legs reach cruising rhythm quickly, but even so, I won't take a break today; I want to get away from this place of human distress as quickly as possible.

The ground becomes more and more sandy. By the end of the day, it's nothing more than a trap that closes around the wheels of my cart. I set up camp. I'm happy to be back home in nature, alone once again. It took a sustained effort to get here, and in my mouth is the taste of satisfaction resulting from physical exertion. I put up my tent and enjoy my first cup of tea of the day. The moon is just visible on the horizon but night hasn't yet come. It's as though the moon is eager to show off her

curves. She is majestic. I leave my tent open all night. As captivated as ever, I can't pass up the show playing out before my
eyes. I'll be her most loyal spectator until late in the night, until
sleep comes to find me.

At dawn I have a hard time waking up, and yet I must leave.
That day I push, I pull, I sweat. The sand eats my wheels, it's
deep enough to slow me down and give me a rough time of it.
Suddenly, an all-terrain vehicle comes silently out from behind a
rock. *Hmm*, that's strange. I'm on guard. When it catches up to
me, the Mongolian driver stops and the two passengers speak to
me in English. They're geologists; the man is Italian and around
sixty years old, and the woman appears to be Mongolian and in
her forties. They ask me if I've seen any ninjas. I learn that ninjas are independent, illegal gold diggers who travel at night and
hide during the day so they can dig. They warn me that the Gobi
Desert is crawling with them. The driver takes out a bottle of
vodka stuck in his door and decides to offer up a round. He fills
a little glass with liquor, but no one wants any. So he decides to
drink for all of us before getting back on the road! It doesn't really matter to me whether or not he's sober on this open plain,
it won't change much either way. I watch as they drive away,
thinking that they could be ninjas themselves. Why would
geologists be worried about ninjas if not to find out where they
are? Or to sneak by without being seen by other ninjas? It
couldn't matter less to me, and I walk on.

I stop that night at the foot of some minor hills that resem-
ble mini dunes. The vegetation that grows in the cracks seems
to be a sort of wild morning glory—leathery, creeping, with a

few thorns here and there. I take a closer look at this greenery, yellowed by the sun, when I catch sight of the tracks of delicate little legs etched in the sand. Tiny creatures live here? I follow the tracks and find their burrow. I'm filled with wonder: how can these little beings survive here? For 360 degrees all around me, there's nothing—no water, no sound. For once even the wind has died down.

I take off my shoes and bury my bare feet in the fine sand. Cooling relief spreads throughout my entire body. It feels so good here, far from humans. I stay in this position, let go, and breathe. It's been a long time since I allowed myself a moment like this with Mother Nature. I recharge my batteries. My perspective on the outside world has changed, without my really being able to explain it. I seem to be operating with an expanded consciousness.

Suddenly, a little thought creeps into my mind: *Don't forget about those who live in the desert!*

I immediately pull my feet from the sand and set them down on my tarp. Almost instantly, a tiny, moving thing to my right catches my eye as it skitters under my tarp. Curious, I gently lift the tarp and find a translucent scorpion like nothing I've ever seen before, taunting me with its arched tail. That is definitely interesting, and before I do anything else, I put my shoes back on and put up my tent. I really don't want creatures getting into my backpack, which is likely to happen if I don't put away my things. Later, during the night, they'll come out of their hiding places, climb all over me and voyage across my face. Usually when this happens, it's big ants or spiders, and it doesn't bother me, but with scorpions, it's a little annoying. . . .

These animals are, however, fascinating. Take, for example, the way they eat: scorpions don't eat, they drink. Let me explain: first they cut their prey into small bits and make a pile. Then, they spit a digestive liquid that transforms the pile into a mush that they suck up and swallow. In the chapter on habits and customs, one also finds the fairly surprising behavior of the female. She carries her young on her back until they're fifteen days old, which is when their armor hardens. After that, it's "every man for himself," since the female scorpion eats her young.

This is the first time since I left that I've ended a day peacefully. Sitting cross-legged, I make myself a cup of tea while the horizon changes color, from pastel blue to a delicate pink. The essence of this day's end contains everything I could want.

The days slip by. I appreciate each minute of them. I love this isolation, I love the beauty of this desert. I've always felt that life doesn't give something for nothing, and that everything has a cost. This makes me savor the magic of these short moments even more. If you arrived at my camp right now, you would find me with a contented smile. You would certainly ask me why I was so happy and I'd respond, "I'm in the right place at the right time, that's all. I feel it, I know it." My heart is breathing with Earth.

In the early morning, small, high-pitched, plaintive cries pull me from my sleep. I stretch my body like a cat—my muscles are talking to me. I realize that the sun has been up for some time. I've slept a restorative, uninterrupted sleep. Mechanically, I unseal my nomad capsule and take my first look at the day outside. The spectacle I find there is timeless. All around my tent, camels graze the rare tufts of green. There are about fifteen of these animals. The baby camels emit never-ending, high-pitched, plaintive sounds that pierce the air, while the adults move about gracefully, soundlessly, with movements that exude ease. They slip through the scenery. I can feel all the marks left on me by the sustained effort of the past months stamped out before this scene of life.

From the next day on I'm once again at the mercy of the wind, exposed and vulnerable like the tumbleweed that the wind carries where it will. I know that the storms won't last, that the wind will one day stop, and that each step is one step closer to my destination. I've woven myself a second skin made of fibers of hope. I'm keenly aware of how badly I need this protection. I'll have to patiently ache, take one step at a time, no more and no less. I know deep down that one day, in two years or more, I'll be back at my own little tree in the south of Australia, where I'll put down my pack for good. For the moment, I have to learn to let things go, to endure without being able to control.

But all this will soon undergo a change in intensity.

It happens at the heart of a violent and unforeseeable storm.

One afternoon, the milky-blue sky suddenly changes color. Five short minutes are all it takes for it to transform itself into a monster of big, fat, dark grey clouds, lit up here and there by muffled electric discharges. I organize myself, I'm all too familiar with what comes next. I'm ready, curled up in the fetal position on the ground. My head in my hands, I prepare to withstand another of the numerous tests that Mother Nature seems to enjoy throwing in my path. The rain comes first in gusts and slaps my face. It's followed by a raft of lightning flashes. I start to shiver with cold and with dread, the ground trembles and takes it. Flat, the ground seems infinite, rolling out for miles around without a tree, without a rock. The lightning won't be attracted to a tree or another protuberance as it usually is, in this case it will strike at random. I know that at this moment, Zeus is playing Russian roulette with me. I just need to get through it and block it out, that's all. I clench my teeth. I'm okay! It will pass. . . .

I withstand it alright, but I can't block it out. So with everything I have left, I start to scream at this ridiculous storm, a habit I'll keep for the rest of my expedition. I shout, "Really? That's all you've got for me? I'm sure you can do better than that. Come on!"

My voice is quickly swallowed up by the thunder that's booming again, a bit too close for my taste. I feel the ground tremble beneath my body. I look quickly at my cart and my pack, which are a mere three hundred yards away, and wish that I had put more distance between us. Both pieces of gear have metal frames that could attract lightning. The ground continues to shake at regular intervals, and despite everything, I find the spectacle beautiful. But I've had enough and I close my eyes for a moment. My body shudders again; I abandon myself to this earth and ask it for protection. And it's at this exact moment that it happens. Suddenly, something happens, I'm not able to explain it, it's as though my body no longer belongs to me, as though I am the lightning, the ground, the clouds, and the rest. I'm all of this at the same time, without distinction. I become aware that my little tree in Australia is not an end in itself. My destination is within me, everything is within me because I'm connected to the all and to everything.

My outlook is changed forever, just then, in the space of a second or two. A bit like someone put thousands of little windows all over my body, enabling me to feel and understand the exterior. But also like my interior merged with the world beyond. It changes everything. In that moment, I feel in my gut the precious bond between each living cell. It's beyond words.

I pull myself together and look at the sky. Far away, lightning bolts still tear at the dark, but the storm has distanced itself. I stand up. I'm in a state of shock, my body no longer seems to be my own; truly, something has changed in me. It will take me several days after these events to be able to function normally, by which I mean, walk, put up camp, eat, sleep, wake up, eat, pack up camp, and all the rest.

Today I'm just here, stretched out beneath this small shrub that gives off so little shade. It's decorated with spines well-adapted to this hostile environment made up of wind, sand, and heat. For 360 degrees around, everything is caramel brown and dull mouse grey, a mix of sand and dry rock. I'm here, just here, my eyes rest on the horizon, whether it likes it or not. I know where I am on my detailed map, I'm not lost. And yet I know that the route will still be long. My body has given everything, my eyelids close as if to forget. I've wound a patched, khaki-colored scarf around my face; I'm so tired. All my clothes are the color of sand, the wind's seen to that. My skin is dirty, my lips dry, my hands, dirty and rough. They're so sturdy you'd think they belonged to a man. The Gobi is empty, or, more accurately, it's a place where the earth has been stripped bare.

If I could look down on this scene from 150 feet in the air, like a bird, I'd be just a small, insignificant dot in the emptiness. The desert's magic doesn't really belong to the desert, but to the space that it contains. Here there is nothing, no possible protection, no dunes, just nothing. None of the things that were found in my previous life could be useful to me here. The feeling of being alone in the middle of this emptiness is surprising at first. Then after long days, long months of walking with no expectations of any kind, things transform themselves of their own accord. I permanently adapt to my environment, which becomes instantly familiar. Is this why I find myself precisely here? Is it to shed the habits of my old life? Is it indeed the only way to maintain my life's internal fire?

I will wait for the sun, far away, to sink before I walk again.

For miles around, I see no one, not a sign of the presence of a yurt. The ground is a golden yellow and stretches out like cake batter, all the way to where the horizon line becomes blurry. I sniff the air and close my eyes. I breathe, again and again. I jump for joy, I'm finally alone! I pick up my video camera, explain where I am, my euphoria. I try to find words for what I'm experiencing, but they don't reflect the spontaneity I feel. Deserts push away those who don't know how to see, who require entertainment and bustle. That leaves only a few passionate nature lovers and adventurers of spirit, as well as some Chinese prospectors who rush to the doors of these giants of sand and stone.

Internal clock

I always navigate by instinctively finding my position in the landscape. For reasons I don't really understand, I can find north without a compass or GPS. From there, the sun helps me find east and west, while the south is obvious. A recent study demonstrates that a few nights of camping are enough to reset your internal clock and reduce your level of stress.

As for me, I understood very early that it was imperative that I understand my body and that I take care of it. Staying healthy often translates into respecting our body's rhythm and constantly repositioning in order to find balance. There's a way to stay healthy while staying far from doctors. It relies on an action that we all do, and better yet, it's free: we must sleep, sleep as long as our body tells us to. Three-quarters of the population watches television before going to sleep, and thirty percent of us regularly take sleep aids. To stay connected to my environment when I'm not on expedition, I always sleep according to nature's rhythm. I don't close my curtains, so I wake up naturally with the first light of day. Everything functions on the same rhythm, all of nature: animals, tides, the moon, etc.

For reasons that still escape me, we arrogantly assume that we're detached from nature. And yet, everything is plainly before our eyes. No one told us a story about the existence of the moon, the sun, the tides, the night, the day—it's all right in front of us!

The key word is *balance*. Our bodies and spirits need to find our life's sustaining light. But how? I suggest small changes, one step at a time. We can guide our life's choices, our life's places, and consequently, our activities. We need to stop "prewashing" our brains with images emitted by a cathode ray tube before going to bed.

Instead, let's listen to our bodies breathe, let's take a few conscious steps per day, let's smile, let's spend a few minutes looking at the clouds, greet a passerby, touch the bark of a tree. You see what I'm saying, nothing too complicated or costly. The only luxury that I see is time.

You don't have the time?

And if you reorganized your schedule, cutting out all those catch-all activities that graft themselves onto our lives as though they were indispensable when they aren't? If you left spaces where you could be alone, breathe, make your heart laugh, feel your blood travel throughout your body? Without having to try, you'd scrape off the mud and find your internal voice, your best friend who you've forgotten and who's become tangled up in this pile of nothings.

My body is my own personal laboratory. Each person's body is unique. What works for others might not work for you. Pay attention to your body, make it smile, don't use it as a mere tool. Everything is connected: body, spirit, mind, heart. In my case, I talk to it often, I listen to it, I stretch it, I avoid exposing it to polluted places, sounds, air, and people. Here again, it needs a little of everything in small doses, at certain moments and not at others. It alone can tell you what it needs. Above all, don't lock yourself into any kind of dogma; instead, continually question yourself, test, feel. What's ideal today may not be tomorrow. Impermanence. But are you ready to listen to it? Are you ready to change?

Often the idea of change is more difficult than the change itself.

Nature leaves behind tracks, you just have to puzzle them out to understand her and survive.

Nature can't be read as we are accustomed to reading, but in exactly the opposite way. Nature is read in its entirety, like a scene, a post card. You have to look to understand what's missing, what shouldn't be there, the signs that will lead you to find the clues you're looking for.

The wind often meddles, tampering with your precious clues.

Rain can be your ally; prints will be deeper on wet ground. As for the snow, she records all tracks and, with her white coat, creates excellent acoustics in the forest.

All the details are extremely important: temperature, odor, shadow, instinct, water, sound, space. I end with space because it's been the hardest one for me. To summarize, I'll say that you must be conscious of your environment at each moment. I deepened this reading of nature on my expedition in Australia in 2002–2003 where I traveled 8,700 miles on foot, alone, across the most isolated spaces on the continent in wilderness-survival mode. My question behind this expedition was very simple. I wanted to know, as a white woman, if I could survive in the Australian Outback, where Aborigines have survived for more than sixty thousand years. Seventeen months of walking later,

I successfully finished this incredible expedition, which changed my life forever. I experienced hunger, true hunger. I hunted, for long hours, sometimes returning empty-handed. I learned to be satisfied with nothing when the hunt was unsuccessful. I ate snakes, monitor lizards, rabbits, birds, but also bush potatoes—which aren't easy to find—and witchetty grubs: big, white larvae that hide in the roots of mulga trees, among others. I also sucked the nectar of grevilleas flowers to savor the syrup, being careful not to cut them, instead leaving them on the bush. So I can answer my initial question, YES, it is possible. But more than anything, I pushed my desire to know my body and my mental and physical capacities incredibly far. I took on my expeditions with the same curiosity that's moved me since childhood, the curiosity of the unknown and an endless thirst for life in all its forms.

My greatest fascination concerns the functioning of the human body.

People often ask me what I think about when I walk. Well, I don't think, I live! There are moments for reflection and others for movement.

Movement is lifesaving; it calls everything into question, everything that's around us that lives, breathes, moves—we humans included. Nothing is constant as we imagine it. Everything evolves with each second.

Our body needs a delicate balance to function. Give it too much of one thing, no matter how good, and it will lose its equilibrium.

The body shouldn't function frenetically, but like a racing motor it should be fine-tuned. Eastern philosophies link the body to the spirit, while we get stuck only on the body's mechanics.

I wanted to experiment, to push, to feel my body, to measure the impact of my spirit on my body and, inversely, experience the impact of my performance on my mental state.

My first encounter with *Canis lupus chanco*

Since I first encountered Mongolians, they've always told me terrifying stories about wolves, warning me of the danger. The Mongolian wolf is called *Canis lupus chanco*. Naturally, the wolf takes from the nomads' herds those animals that are old, sick, and wounded, cleansing the herd of illness, which strengthens the genetic line. The wolf is respected by the nomads, but not well-loved. Normally, when I encounter a sober nomad on horseback, one of his first questions is, "Where are you going?" followed by, "Have you seen any wolves?"

After months in this territory, I'm starting to be able to express myself, which has required mastering fifty words of their complex language—enough to have a conversation composed of a few handfuls of words. When I relate my different encounters with wolves, I sense their gaze become focused. At times I even notice impatient movements, very unusual for them. This comes across as repeated gestures that seem nondescript, but which don't escape me. A question is burning on their lips: Where did you see the wolves?

I always tell them the wrong direction, knowing that the few wolves that remain will be taken down by a bullet from a predator greedy for their strength and their organs, which are used in shamanic medicine, but not only that. The information that I've been able to glean on the subject of the wolf is meager. But it seems clear that when someone kills a wolf, the strength of the wolf is transferred to the person who dispatched him. And then there's the other facet of wolf hunting that's linked to the neighbor to the south: in China, there's a huge traffic in organs—intestines, bile, etc., that are sold for the price of gold for their aphrodisiacal virtues. It's a demand that completely escapes me and one that no one really wants to talk about. The Chinese are responsible for the extinction of so many wild animals.

The Mongolians ardently try to scare me with their improbable wolf stories. I try to make use of the occasion to ask them constructive questions, such as, "How should you react when a wolf is nearby?" "What should you do if it approaches?" "Is there a particular period when it's most dangerous?"

Often the nomads seem disconcerted by my questions. I try to phrase them differently, asking what they do when faced with a wolf. This quickly loosens tongues, and responses pour forth. It can give way to hilarious mimed scenes, sometimes even real theatrical performances in which the whole family participates, with dazzling sound effects. All of these scenes have one thing in common: a rifle. Often the scene ends right on the ground in a huge collective laugh. When everyone's calmed down, I tell them that I don't have a rifle. *Hmm!* Often the head of the family looks at me darkly. I can read his thoughts: *You think you'll escape the wolves without a gun?*

This is the fruit of my survey in the steppe of northern and central Mongolia: if I run into a wolf, I was advised to crouch down and look the wolf in the eyes, facing it. Others told me to make myself as big as possible to scare it. Still others implored me never to look a wolf in the eyes. But everyone had one piece of advice in common: "Make a fire." I'm satisfied with this last technique, which seems simple and logical. There's just one little problem: there's little or no wood in the steppe.

They're howling . . .

I'm finally at the foot of the rocks. I get there just in time before the sun sets. The horizon is colored in intense orange streaks; I'm satisfied and smiling. Three days ago, I chose these huge rock walls as a navigational point of reference in this desert where everything looks so similar. It's taken time for my senses to once again get used to the real desert I love so much. The space fascinates me, I feel like I'm breathing anew, finally free, emancipated from my human landmarks in these zones where the smallest movement seems to echo in the void. The void here is as though full, my movements are more conscious than ever. These gigantic, round monsters that seem to come straight up out of the ground intrigue me. I put down my things. I'm exhausted, and yet I feel so light without my backpack. Regardless of my fatigue, I go exploring. I walk along the rock, my fingers brushing this craggy barrier that seems like an enormous nest in the middle of the desert. I imagine rocks as libraries of time, nothing can destroy them. For the most part, they've been here for centuries, they've seen so many things. It's why I respect them, and I never forget to greet them.

I notice that the back of this rocky formation is the continuation of the wall that I've followed here. It's shaped like an egg chopped off at the summit, with a tiny little gap to the west. The interior is hollow, in places round rocks appear in the middle, and I can make out vegetation. I'm intrigued, I imagine that the interior must be a real paradise. The rock is smooth, without holds big enough to climb, and the gap is at the summit. I'm frustrated; I would have liked to discover this place that, from my vantage point, has all the elements of an oasis.

I return to my camp. I need to make something to eat, since the light is fading. I fall asleep like a baby.

I wake up suddenly and sit up ramrod straight; this surprises me. I look at the time. My Tissot T-Touch watch shows four o'clock in the morning. I find this situation a bit unusual and try to figure out what could have woken me so instinctually. Outside my tent the wind has fallen, there's no sound. There must be a reason, I think. My two ears wide open, I wait for sounds in the still night. After an hour, my eyelids are finally closing when I'm awakened by the howling of wolves. They're right near my tent, close by. I freeze, smiling. And yet a shiver travels over my skin, adrenaline has seized my body. I don't move. I know that the cloth of my tent won't protect me from a pack of wolves. I'd like to howl like a wolf, too, to reply. But given my circumstances, I prefer to stay quiet and savor the close quarters with these survivors. I'm so lucky to live this moment. . . . *Thank you, thank you* . . .

At dawn, I open my tent and contemplate the imposing rock. There's no doubt, this is where they live. I'm happy that this fortress protects them. I'll keep the location secret, to preserve them a bit longer from men and their follies.

The long night of Mandal-Oovo

I'm coming from the north, just ninety miles from my resupply point. My cart endlessly sinks into the sand and it's thanks to my superhuman efforts that the miles sneak by, although not fast enough for my taste.

I arrive at this dusty village, behind me are ten days in the desert, sand storms, and soft sand. I go directly to the store and ask for a place where I can sleep. They shoo me away with the backs of their hands and a "*Barko,*" so I start knocking on doors to find the public baths, then a room or a yurt for the night. I'm completely worn out by this long crossing: it's been days and days since I've had sufficient rations of food or water. I come upon a woman walking nonchalantly in flip-flops, with Barbie-pink nail polish. She directs a subtle movement in my direction and I follow her to a shack to which she has the key, without a single word exchanged between us. Inside, the place accommodates men who look at me out of the corners of their eyes. There's no toilet—not even a hole in the back of the courtyard—and no running water. She gives me a room with no lock and no bed. Just an empty room. I shoot her a look that says, "Come on, now!" A smile at the corner of her lips, she shows me another room with a bed and a chest of drawers. A nod of my head is enough, I pay her and let myself fall on the bed. As soon as she pockets the money, the woman disappears.

I dash to the public bath, which is a square building at the back of the village, a legacy of the Soviet regime. I go into one of the five extremely narrow shower stalls. I wonder how those Mongolian men and women on the corpulent side fit into this confined space. I giggle and conclude that only the skinny ones wash.

Boiling water squirts from the wall, through a short iron pipe. I hold myself with one hand against the rough masonry and let the restorative water flow over my bruised body. I come out exhausted and almost clean, having left in the shower my sweat and my long days of walking. I open the iron door and put down my 2,000 tugriks of Mongolian currency, and the caretaker takes the money without lifting her head and continues the back and forth of her nail file. Her silence speaks volumes. In an excellent mood, I ironically thank her in her language for the very nice conversation we didn't have. She doesn't look up.

I return to the shack taking slow, small steps. The wind takes this opportunity to once again fling dust that sticks to my wet skin and irritates my tired eyes. Now that I've let go of the tension, my body is barely able to walk; it's winning out and telling me that it can't move anymore. Cramps engulf my legs, I can't lift my arms. I barricade myself more or less securely in my room. I'll pee in my plastic bottle that I've cut the top off of. Night hasn't yet fallen, nevertheless the music and the Mongolian cacophony has already begun. Throughout the night, drunk people pass in front of the shack and then come back the other way. Music turned all the way up blasts from various cars using the front gate as a departure point for their round-trips. Bottles are smashed against the walls, voices shout, people fight, what a racket! Cars start, footsteps of people I can't see stop at each door. They knock at all the doors, and I can hear that some are forced open. When they arrive at my door, I hold my breath. They beat against it so hard that the door bows beneath the blows. I've put the single piece of furniture in the room in front of it—a heavy dresser from the beginning of the century, brown, lacquered, upholstered with candle wax and slashed with knife marks, among other things. I've put my hiking poles across the door to fortify the whole thing. I sit in the dark without saying a word, my pepper spray hidden under my sweater for the surprise effect just in case. Fear knots my stomach, I don't close my eyes all night. I'll never know what they were looking for. Maybe the "Long Nose . . ."

At the first glimmers of day, exhausted by these trademark Mongolian nocturnal events, I leave, deliberately. I'm not going to follow the path that leads south, I'm instead going to go deep into the desert to hide in some thickets of saxaul trees to avoid problems and, above all, to try to stay alive among the barbarians of this steppe.

80th day of expedition

For days I've had this small rise to the south of me in my sights, and today I'm less than three miles from it. Behind this rock, which is a bit more prominent than I'd thought, there's a tourist camp. This is the place I've chosen for my resupply. The light low, I decide to circumvent the rock and arrive from the south. I've lost weight, I'm exhausted by the nighttime attacks, the sand, the lack of sleep and, underlying it all, I'm especially tired of these people. I climb up on a rock from where I can see the plain change color before me. It's wearing a golden tint in the sun. I take off my hat and let the light, end-of-day thermal breeze dry the sweat that's accumulated beneath it. I'm worn out, too thin, and yet I can't take my eyes off the horizon, I feel the wind on my whole body, I'm breathing. Just for an instant, I close my eyes to savor this moment. Today is the eighth of September, the day of my resupply. I move forward between large stones. I'm almost there, but I can't yet see the white yurts of the camp. Night is starting to fall, when suddenly an all-terrain vehicle approaches. The yurts are there, well-hidden at the foot of the rock. The passenger door opens. . . . It's Gregory, my expedition chief!

One tooth later . . .

The resupply replenishes me, body and soul. I have the pleasure of speaking French with Gregory and eating my fill. We also spend a lot of time planning, filming, and refining the enormous job of synchronization that's necessary for an expedition like this. Time passes very quickly, and a few days later, I'm already walking south. The Gobi Desert awaits.

It's then that my teeth start to hurt. At first it doesn't worry me, since I have all the antibiotics necessary to take care of these kinds of infections. But in just a few hours the infection spreads. Half of my swollen face no longer responds to stimulus. I can tell it's serious. The speed with which the infection has progressed is worrisome. I can't plunge into the Gobi Desert like this. I call my contact in charge of my evacuation so I can get medical care. My own mission is to retrace my steps. I walk holding my head; it hurts so much that "the pain eats the bottom of my socks." I arrive, pale, at my destination. An all-terrain vehicle is already there, a Mongolian I don't know opens the door. Meanwhile, in Switzerland, Gregory has informed my sponsors. Monsieur Delarive, one of my principal sponsors, offers to contact his brother who lives in Tokyo, Japan being the closest country capable of caring for a problem like this that doesn't require a visa. After the work of synchronizing all the moving parts, I'm on an airplane and then landing in Tokyo. It's nighttime, the city lights sparkle. I get myself to my hotel, still in my hiking clothes. They give me a room on the seventy-ninth floor. In the elevator I feel like I'm suffocating. I curl up in pain on the bed. It's fair to say that I'm a bit shaken up. The next day is one of the rare Japanese holidays, and yet my sponsor's contact is going to open his clinic just for me.

I leave with a bandage. An abscess had formed beneath a tooth that had undergone a very old, botched root canal. The whole thing got infected and escaped the notice of my dentist during the dental checkup we did before I left, despite the face scan I had done as a precaution. Putting in place a temporary bandage and cleaning the wound has taken care of a large part of the pain. But the bulk of the work remains to be done. He gives me antibiotics and sends me to one of his colleagues who specializes in bone reconstruction and this type of complication. The treatment will last six long and interminable weeks.

I take refuge in the mountains, in Hakuba, in a little cabin in the woods. I'll commute from here for the duration of my treatment, going to the clinic every six days. One important detail: I'm six hours away from Tokyo's public transportation.

During this period, I'm able to Skype with my sponsors whom I keep regularly informed. When complications arise, my sponsors come together to support me. Doctor Rolland-Yves Mauvernay and his son Thierry of Debiopharm bolster me, and in moments of adversity Doctor Mauvernay adds, "Today is when you need us, and here we are, at your side!"

Monsieur Delarive, by phone, adds, "Sarah, life is like that. Push through." Six weeks after my arrival in Japan, I leave with but one thought in my head: to walk.

5. Gobi Desert—Second Attempt

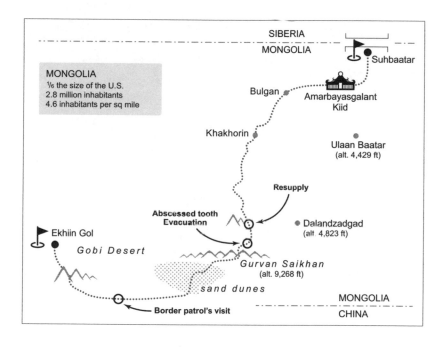

SIBERIA

MONGOLIA

Suhbaatar

MONGOLIA
⅙ the size of the U.S.
2.8 million inhabitants
4.6 inhabitants per sq mile

Bulgan

Amarbayasgalant
Kiid

Khakhorin

Ulaan Baatar
(alt. 4,429 ft)

Resupply

Abscessed tooth
Evacuation

Dalandzadgad
(alt. 4,823 ft)

Ekhiin Gol

Gobi Desert

Gurvan Saikhan
(alt. 9,268 ft)

sand dunes

MONGOLIA

Border patrol's visit

CHINA

Preparation

Gobi Desert, winter

I'M BACK IN MONGOLIA, READY AND IMPATIENT TO START walking again after my forced time off in Japan to treat my abscessed tooth.

At the gigantic outdoor market on the road leading out of town, we were able to get our (very cold) hands (the temperature was -27°F!) on a large aluminum teapot (to melt snow in), a box of big firecrackers (to keep the packs of wolves at bay; in the winter they can be more determined), and various other supplies. Here meat is everywhere, shown off in crude displays. The organs are front and center, while intestines are suspended. Some shoppers look at the cuts with disdain while still trying to talk price. As I'm leaving the meat area, I notice a woman lift the cover off a large pot that's sitting on the ground in front of the stall. A potential buyer leans over to gawk at the contents. Intrigued, I approach and discover with horror the freshly severed head of a dog—a husky—that seems to be looking me straight in the eye!

Meanwhile Bat's colleague motions to me, he's found the sheepskin section.

"Which ones do you want? Look carefully, they're not all the same quality!"

I can't concentrate, I'm haunted by the head of the poor dog. I indicate to the vendor two sheepskins at random. I'm still in shock. I'm freezing, the meat stalls, the intestines, and then the thought of the dog make me sad. I don't speak until we get to the car. We leave, and I don't really know where we're going.

The vehicle stops. Bat, his colleague, and I have arrived in a suburb of Ulaanbaatar at the foot of a series of old, grey, buildings, all crammed together.

The building swallows us up as we go down a stairway. Bat, who's in front, opens an ancient, creaky metal door. Inside, people apply themselves to sewing, folding, gluing. This is where they create beautiful, traditional belts. The workers don't look up, but stay focused on the task at hand. I explain with precise gestures that I'd like them to make me gaiters: they would be made from two pieces of sheepskin, and would completely cover my boots and come all the way up over my knees. I draw a simple sketch that one of the workers looks at for a long time, then nods. We leave this cellar with no ventilation where the glue fumes would have anyone on the floor in a matter of hours.

From Japan, I ordered all the necessary gear to walk and withstand extreme cold. My tent arrives after a few weeks, with a supplementary customs tax of $1,200. It's just the official Mongolian tax, more commonly known here as corruption.

Just two days after our visit to the cellar, we get my sheepskin gaiters, made with thought and precision. They hook in the back and are very easy to attach in the cold wearing gloves.

I have everything I need. I decide to leave the next day for the spot where my last GPS coordinates in the Gobi were taken, from where I was evacuated.

The Mongolian driver and his all-terrain vehicle that Mongolian Expedition mandated drops me off at the tourist camp, just a few miles from my point of evacuation for my abscessed tooth. Here, there's just one family left and twenty empty yurts. The owner receives me and looks at me strangely. After some discussion, they open a yurt just for me. They don't understand what I'm doing here in the winter and alone.

I go into the cold yurt and make a fire that will take hours to heat the interior. Outside, day is falling on the horizon. I'm fascinated. Pale rose and sky blue form on the white that blankets everything. It's the middle of winter and the temperature is -22°F. I carefully spread out my things one last time to be sure that I haven't forgotten anything. I hang up my red and black North Face snowsuit, I fill the Thermos with hot water, etc.

At dawn, the light creeps across the snow, the pink and blue suspended in layers on the surface. Such beauty and serenity! I had already fallen in love with the Gobi in the summer, but now, my preference leans toward winter. I stand openmouthed, captivated by the magic.

This morning, I plunge into the white landscape that seems bottomless, the luminosity is such that it gives no perspective of depth or contour. I'm wearing snow goggles, the kind of sunglasses used for bad weather or while skiing, to offer maximum protection. A chapka is pulled over my head to protect me from wind and cold.

The first night is just a bit chilly; according to my thermometer it's -4°F inside the tent. Outside, a violent wind threatens the tent. I'm so glad to be on the inside, who knows what temperature it is right now on the outside? I don't sleep much that night, holding on to my tent poles from inside all night long, for fear the tent will blow away. On the third night, my tent folds violently beneath lashing gusts of wind, then returns to its initial form. The problem is due in part to the ground, which is completely frozen, so I don't have the advantage of a solid anchoring to the ground.

In the morning of this tumultuous night, I know that I can't go on like this. What if my tent actually ripped?

I evaluate the risks: the nighttime temperature can drop down to between -40° and -49°F with the wind. And what if my tent is ripped to shreds?

In these extreme conditions, what would happen is I'd die of hypothermia. The previous night's fright left a bitter taste in my mouth, the taste of death.

My sight is fixed on this white desert. I must make a decision, and deep down I know that I don't have the choice. I'm sad. I have to stop here.

I'm beaten, and yet I know it's the right decision. I take my satellite phone and call Bat so he can send his contact to pick me up. I give him the exact GPS coordinates. And then I start walking again, it's too cold and I need to move. I'm sure that he'll come and find me easily with my red North Face snowsuit.

I had to adapt my gear, but I hadn't prepared myself to manage

such low temperatures. I later learn that I could have supplied myself
with big, eight-inch-long nails and a large mallet. This would have
allowed me to stabilize the tent on the ground as much as possible.
The snow is eight inches deep in some spots, but it's a light, volatile
snow without structure, so it wouldn't have been possible to use
the snow to hold the tent in place, either. I later learn that in Canada,
they use big, light screws specially devised for these situations, that
easily bore into the frozen ground.

Several hours later, a vehicle approaches slowly. Blaring music
pierces the solitude of this white desert. The driver gives a nod of
his head and loads my things into the back. That night, I'm warm
and comfortable in Dalanzadgad, contemplative before my scalding cup of tea. I still hold the beauty of the white desert within me.
Thoughts run through my mind at a dizzying speed, my gaze is
lost in the void while my spirit deliberates at the speed of light. I'm
going to have to change all my plans, the seasons no longer corre-
spond to the initial plans I made in Switzerland. Everything is out
of sync, including the gear so carefully prepared for my resupplies.

After a long reflection, I decide to follow Mother Nature.
I jump to my feet, and grab my phone to update Switzerland on
my decision about the rest of my expedition.

A new direction is needed

I'll return to the Gobi in another season. I won't admit defeat!
For now, I have to adapt to Mother Nature and not go against
her. To do this, I need to follow the seasons. The time it took to

care for my abscessed tooth threw everything off. So I'm headed to the south of China. I'll walk up through China instead of going down it, to meet back up with the spot where the vehicle came to pick me up.

During the night, I make long phone calls to Switzerland. My expedition chief has to coordinate my arrival in China, with all the appropriate equipment, and send me my visa, authorization, etc. It's all hands on deck; my sponsors must be notified first, and a public statement made. I take care of it in the form of a newsletter that I write during the night. At dawn, the text is in Gregory's in-box with photos and videos. He'll need to format it and send it out as quickly as possible. He'll take care of personally apprising each sponsor of the situation. I've also called my family. They're reassured, everyone's doing well . . . and I talked to my sweet D'Joe. I miss him so much.

Before my departure, I prepare my resupply bags and meticulously prepare my path using aviation maps.

Mongolia: I'm finally where there are no more nomads.

Central Mongolia: The nomads let themselves be lulled by the passage of time in the summer.

Mongolia: My tea break is very important, it's a moment that brings me comfort through contemplation.

Mongolia—Gobi Desert: At the end of the day, if I have time, I film, take pictures, or write.

Resupply: Gregory, my expedition leader.

Credit: Snow Leopard Trust

The photo that my motion-activated camera took.

I hide in culverts.

The first nomad I encountered.

Mongolia: The beginning was hard.

Mongolia—Gobi Desert: -27° F.

Mongolia—Gobi Desert: He smoked a cigarette and continued on his way.

Mongolia—Gobi Desert: One step at a time, I move closer to my destination.

Gobi Desert: From where I am, I identify the spot where I'll be able to cross this chain of mountains.

Gobi Desert: An umbrella is always among my gear.

Gobi Desert: That morning, I open my tent . . . what a wonderful surprise!

Gobi Desert: I invite him to have some tea.

Gobi Desert: The singing dunes; a water source crosses them.

Laos: I leave the Namtha River and plunge into the jungle.

China: I hide from prying eyes.

Thailand: My arrival at Ayutthaya—Wat Phukhao Thong.

Laos: I go down the Namtha River in a canoe; the jungle is dense.

The Australian bush, with saltbush (*Atriplex*) shrubs and salmon gum (*Eucalyptus salmonophloia*).

My camp, isolated from everything, in Northern Australia.

The wild cattle owned by Frank and his nephew.

My D'Joe, who walked 6,200 miles by my side in 2002–2003.

Arrival at my resupply in Northern Australia.

Southern Australia.

I stop three miles from the end, and with a few twigs, I make my last tea.

Without my cart, this wouldn't have been possible.

I'm a mile from my destination . . . the helicopter flies in circles above me.

Credit: Lynn Webb

May 17, 2013: Arrival at my little tree on Nullarbor Plain, Southern Australia—after three years.

6. China

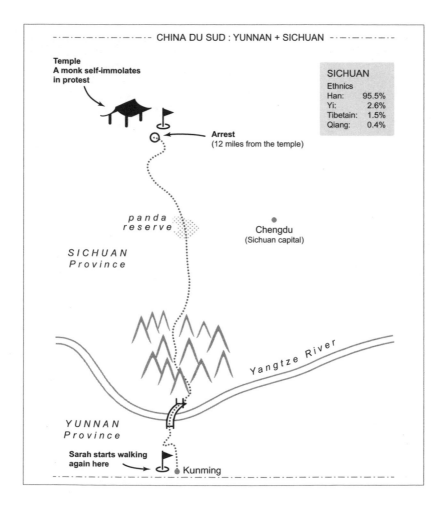

CHINA DU SUD : YUNNAN + SICHUAN

**Temple
A monk self-immolates
in protest**

Arrest
(12 miles from the temple)

SICHUAN	
Ethnics	
Han:	95.5%
Yi:	2.6%
Tibetain:	1.5%
Qiang:	0.4%

*panda
reserve*

Chengdu
(Sichuan capital)

*SICHUAN
Province*

Yangtze River

*YUNNAN
Province*

**Sarah starts walking
again here**

Kunming

Kunming—Yunnan, January 2011

I JUST ARRIVED IN KUNMING, THIS CITY OF THREE MILLION overexcited inhabitants. All my senses are solicited, between the noise of the streets, the odors of human activities, the mobile vendors, the old ladies in front of their stalls, the red and gold emblems. Slim-silhouetted Asian bodies move nervously and anonymously through space, contrasting in every way with the gentle nonchalance of the Mongolians.

In the north of Mongolia, on a dusty road, I had met Mathias and Véronique, a couple with peaceful smiles and laughing eyes. We were surprised by our common presence at this end of Earth. They had left Germany and had traveled across all of eastern Europe before traveling to Asia. They'd done it all on bicycle. Amazing! What an effort. I had only to look at their load to imagine their trek. We drank a cup of tea sitting on the side of the road, chatted, and then after two hours, we each continued on our respective way, promising to keep in touch by e-mail.

After arriving in Kunming, I sent them a message asking if things were going well on their end. I told them about the last six months of my journey. I received their response an hour later: they told me that they were in Kunming where they were recuperating from a long and difficult crossing of China. Consequently, they were impatiently waiting to see me somewhere in the city.

We decide to meet in an old-fashioned little tea shop next to a lake. When we meet, I'm moved to see them again; so many roads have been traveled since we've seen each other. We drink a toasted barley tea and our conversations center around China and our arduous experiences. The next day, they invite me to meet them at their guesthouse. I meet up with them late morning. It's only a few degrees inside, as the rooms aren't heated. We'd all prefer to be outside, so we sit out on the small patio. Mathias repairs a tire while Véronique is happily absorbed in her knitting. Our conversations are accompanied by steaming hot tea and a bag of mandarin oranges that we eat without restraint. Suddenly Mathias stands up, he's just remembered a detail and explains that I absolutely need to have a certain type of map that I won't find anywhere but here. He tells me he knows where to find the office that sells them. In a city of three million people where everything is written in Mandarin, I can't refuse his offer. He quickly takes off. A few hours later, he reappears with a sort of road atlas full of Chinese characters about the size of a hardcover novel. Thanks, Mathias!

We part ways the next day, as it's time for all of us to go. Véronique and Mathias are continuing due south via Laos and

Thailand. As for me, I have before me a country to cross of which I know neither language nor culture. I leave confidently. What could possibly happen that would compare to the misadventures I had in Mongolia?

Pigs' destiny in Chinese territory

I fall into my rhythm, my pack full of good things and fresh produce that I missed so much in Mongolia. I plunge into the Chinese countryside, far from the bustle of the city. I need to get my bearings. Everything is different here, language, nature, people, sounds, smells, to say nothing of the food. It can't be worse than in Mongolia where the most exciting vegetable was a potato. As a vegetarian, I still laugh to think how I jubilated over a Mongolian potato—who would have thought!

I trudge over these dirt paths, the small towns go by and they all look alike. The dirt roads have ruts on either side where all the garbage of the village flows out. It's a paradise for fat pigs and ducks. At dawn, as the water buffalo are led out to the fields, they observe me with astonishment. These slices of life are simple and banal. And yet, it's as though I'm entering a new world. From behind my sunglasses nothing escapes me—the children who silently study me between the bars of the doorways, the bunches of corn suspended from the eaves of houses, a woman washing her long, black hair, leaning over a large aluminum bowl, the marking of family shields on freshly whitewashed walls. I let myself be seduced by what I see, by this rural world. I let gazes rest on me, dogs sniff me, thin, silent men stare suspiciously at me.

The terrain is uneven, the temperature perfect. I advance along a road that's turned into a path. The valley narrows, I have to observe, to feel. My maps are basic road maps, as it's forbidden in China to have topographic maps. I've decided to rediscover my old senses; I'm going to cross this land with my compass and basic maps. This day, around noon, I arrive at the entrance of a small village that sprawls and stretches all the way up to the summit of a little mountain. The sight that awaits me there freezes me in my tracks. In each yard, bloody pig heads are stuck on tree branches, which are leafless in accordance with the season. And on the side of the road, no pigs greet me as usual with decorous squeals. In the gutters on either side of the road, blood flows in streams. Old women raise their metal hatchets in the air, in slow motion. They smile. The noise of the cleavers carving up the animals makes me jump. Death meets my gaze everywhere my eyes come to rest. Another pig is being forcefully pulled by five men, dragged like a sack of potatoes. It's screaming bloody murder. I keep walking without lifting my head, I stare at my shoes, and I take exactly eight steps before the squealing stops short. In front of each house, on the road, a table made of boards is placed and each family is killing its pigs. Everyone is covered in blood, intestines are emptied and hung up here and there. I continue, but in contemplation of those being sacrificed. Peace be with them, take care of them.

I'm in Han territory, and people look at me darkly, suspiciously. They don't talk to me, in fact they ignore me, and that's just fine with me. I stop occasionally at the village grocery to buy a small bag of rice, garlic, eggs, sweet puffed rice cakes, flour, a bit of oil, and sugar. For fresh produce, I have to rely on chance. They're only sold at the market that's held once a week or once a month.

I study a few words of civility. Most of all, I observe and memorize gestures that will serve me throughout my stay in China. I learn numbers in sign language. With the help of my hands, I come to be able to communicate wordlessly with anyone, regardless of their ethnic group. After a while, I'm able to bargain in silence with the old women. They're quick, I have to carefully follow their gestures. These moments with these women with wrinkled skin and an easy smile are possibly the best I've spent. It seems that their view of life is more open and wise than that of the young.

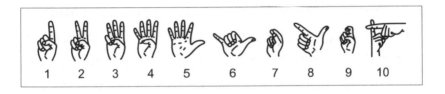

I forge ahead blindly, without a topo map. I can't pronounce the name of the next village since it's in Mandarin, and I can't read it either. Because of this, I can't really find where I am on my maps, but I'm confident, the direction is true, I'm going north. I find the situation quite refreshing. Having to count on data other than my maps adds flavor to my days. I like being in the dark, not knowing how many miles I am from the next village, the next water source. Despite all this, I'm very careful: I'm not in a desert, but I still fill my water containers every chance I get. I protect myself by sleeping as far as possible from villages, in the forest or in a rice paddy suspended in the terraces. I've become an expert in camouflage. I never stay in the villages, I slip into the scenery. My hat is pulled firmly down over my head and my sunglasses on my nose, my hair is hidden under a stretchy cotton band the color of sand; not a strand of hair is visible. I wash only rarely—the occasions don't really present themselves—and I don't look for them either, it's far from being my priority. The valleys are deepening and I find myself in front of real passes to climb, with gravity-defying rice paddies on the side of the slope. I have to pull my cart, no matter what the terrain. It's become an extension of my body. I sweat, I push, the effort is substantial.

I've been chipping away at this pass since yesterday morning, thinking that I'm almost at the summit, without ever getting there. But now, deliverance is near. Indeed, ten minutes later, I've succeeded. Sweat drips down my face. I mechanically take off my glasses, still out of breath. And stop short, open-mouthed, before the vision that stretches before me. A stark panorama of jagged mountains with bare, rocky peaks is outlined against the horizon. Before me is an enormous void, a valley, at the bottom of which flows a disproportionately narrow ribbon of river. From the other side of the river rises this rocky range sliced up as though with a knife, the way one cuts a slice from a birthday cake. My eyes try to find the path that will lead me out of this situation. I find it winding like a piece of spaghetti down to the bottom of the valley. I set forth confidently into this furious descent that I estimate to be a 6,500-foot change in altitude. I won't reach the banks of the river until the following day at noon.

From the east I enter this village that seems to have its feet in the water, yet also provides access to a bridge. My legs are burning, my feet are jelly. I walk backward for three hundred yards to take the pressure off my muscles and tendons, when violent detonations tear through the valley. They're followed by a second salvo, then another until the bottom of the valley is buried in a cloud of powder or whatever it is that comes out of these series of agricultural firecrackers. It takes me a moment to grasp the situation, and it's the villagers' joy and the red and gold decorations that make me understand that it's the Chinese new year, the year of the rabbit. It's February 3, 2011. Smiling, I cross the gigantic red and black bridge suspended above the Yangtze River. People are coming from far away, as couples or whole families, sometimes four to a scooter, to boom in the new year. This valley floor, the people, the fireworks—I find all of it oppressive. I scramble up the other side as quickly as possible, a 6,500-foot climb. On New Year's day I set foot on the other side of the river, in the Sichuan province.

The months that follow see me struggling mightily with these mountains so particular to Sichuan. Hiking has been my life for more than twenty years—a long time. It's my deepest passion, it's what makes my heart sing. The villages become more spaced out, roads have become paths that only small motorcycles travel. Then one day, I'm at the bottom of a valley with a single path, a single possible direction, that unfortunately does not lead north. I fill my cart with rice, with those precious packets of instant coffee that propel me forward, and with flour that allows me to make little pancakes. I stay a moment sitting in front of the only grocers in the village; the sun is there and caresses me with its warmth. I'm grateful. At the communal spring, I fill each of my water containers without spilling a drop. I can't wait around, I need to put some distance between the village and my camp for the night. I get down to the task at hand—climbing the summit before me—to see more clearly and to set a navigational point. I'll decide on my next destination once I've arrived at the top. For the moment, I advance along this straight little dirt path, tamped down by its users over the years. I've gained an ability to adapt myself and make familiar the things around me. So, I love this old path, I feel it deeply, even if I don't know where it's leading me. I stop a moment to wipe the sweat dripping from my forehead. My cart is heavy with water. Meanwhile, on the slope below, a woman is coming with two buckets hanging from a pole balanced across her shoulders. She bends down, keeping her load steady; the two buckets touch the ground at the same time. It's an art to balance heavy loads like she's doing. She methodically deposits the pig manure that they contain. The odor is unbearable. My eyes move to the steep slope before I ease back into my walking rhythm. When I reach the summit, the sun is starting to fall gently behind the mountains. I'm far from odors, far from noises. I take my pack from my back and collapse. I'm soaking wet, the climb took substantial effort. I like the taste of satisfaction that mixes with my saliva at the end of this day. A sort of indescribable pleasure that slips in small doses from the pain that the hiker must tame. Before me, a parade of mountains and valleys by the dozen follow one after the other, without apparent order or linearity. The intensity of color fades on the farthest summits. They all seem to be the same height, it's surprising! If I plunge into this jumble of mountains, summits, and valley floors, it will take me weeks to come out, and who knows if I'll find food there? Will it be possible for me to continue going north? So many questions run through my mind. . . . The horizon becomes misty, the temperature has dropped, I put up my tent. I'm not hungry, which is fortunate. Good night, China!

Black is his skin, long is his nose . . .

It's been ten days since I made the decision to head off into these mountains, and I've only seen a few people on motorbikes. I've rationed my reserves for fear of not finding anywhere to resupply. I like this spare landscape. The path that follows the ridge veers eastward, just below a cream-colored cliff. From where I am, I can't see the way out. I stop, I make some tea, the pine trees keep me from reading the scenery. There is absolutely no reason for me to go in this direction, especially if there's no way to get through, as I'm certainly blocked by this cliff that's in the form of a natural cirque. As I drink my tea, I become confident that there will surely be an intersection, a fork at the base of this cliff that will lead me to the other side of the mountain. I start walking again, it's the beginning of the afternoon. I arrive at the rock, but to my great surprise, there isn't a path leading off to the west. Rather, in front of me is a masterpiece. I can't believe it.

Clearly, nothing is impossible in China! A tunnel is carved in the rock, as though by a giant grub through the earth. Slowly, I start in. The ground is uneven, my cart bounces and tips over. I concentrate. My pack touches the rock above me—it's not very high—so I have to bend my knees. I move forward, hoping that the rock has been cleared all the way to the top. The path is shallower here; I move ahead one step at a time. I wonder about the people who made this path: what an enormous task! The cliff in which the path is carved plunges straight down over several hundred yards. After some cold sweats, I arrive at the other side of this natural cirque that the path leads through. I look behind me and smile, hoping that I won't have to cross it again going the other way. From where I am, the path is damp, unstable. I focus and keep moving, full of determination, when suddenly it changes direction and rises vertically for several yards, opening onto a plateau. Before me stand a handful of little earthen houses, with women squatting peacefully in front of small fires. They turn potatoes, leaning against the adobe wall; very thin yellow dogs are lying here and there. I walk slowly, hoping not to startle them. Suddenly, they turn and look at me. I make a small, calm gesture so as not to scare them, but screams of terror immediately ring out. Women and children come out from everywhere, they're completely panicked, they yell and run in all directions as though there were an earthquake, not knowing where to take refuge. I cross the village in the same rhythm, ignoring their screams to reassure them, even if I think that at this point, it would take a lot more than a long explanation to calm them down.

I draw away from the village, I'm sad to have frightened them so much. More than half a mile away, I set up camp on a low berm just big enough to accommodate my tent. Night will soon fall. Sitting cross-legged, I'm cooking my rice when suddenly, they approach like a funeral procession. Leading it is their chief, an imposing figure by the energy he radiates. A felt cape attached to his neck by a string covers his whole body. As I study him from head to toe, it's his skin that holds my attention. It's extremely wrinkled from the sun, and so dark that it's almost a deep reddish-black. But what strikes me the most is his nose, long and slender. His other features don't look Asian, but seem to come straight from North Africa. I notice a small leather pouch hanging from his neck. He gestures to me. I stand up, which causes the fifty people in rags watching me to step back, fearful and tense. I'm a hundred yards from their spot down below. Their chief holds himself ramrod straight with a calm, yet hostile expression. I explain my presence here with gestures practiced countless times. He doesn't understand. I inform him that I'll leave tomorrow. He looks at me for a long moment. I feel like I'm in Rome, in the Colosseum, waiting while the lions roar behind me. I wait. After an eternity, in complete silence, he decides to return to the village, his subjects at his heels. I have time to eat my rice and drink a cup of tea before I hear voices down below. People are cutting branches, and while I can't see them, I hear machete chops and then nothing. A few minutes later, the familiar smell of a dense and bitter smoke invades my camp. Some of the wood they're burning is still green, producing this acrid smoke. I start coughing, and soon I can't see anything. I have to move, despite the night which is a mere few minutes from total darkness. I've understood their strategy, I quickly break camp and set out into the night, far from here. . . .

The Sichuan mountains are home to some fifty-six ethnic minorities living in China, including the Yi, Lisus, Dais, Bais, Miaos, and others. They each have their own language and culture, which are entirely different from those of the Han who represent the majority of Chinese people. During the weeks I move through these mountains, I have the occasion to interact with these minorities. The isolation resulting from the complexity and inaccessibility of the mountains still protects them from the outside world. I'm fascinated by their elegant beauty, their eyes so often at once laughing and knowing.

The weeks that follow my first encounter with ethnic minorities are marked by a succession of nights spent at magnificently wild camps between 8,000 and 10,000 feet above sea level, entire days walking in pine forests, and dramatic crossings of virgin rivers. At the foot of a stream, at the top of a pass, or at the edge of a path, I run into colorfully dressed women from different groups. Their clothing reveals their social status, their ethnic origin, and all sorts of subtleties that escape me. With a single look and without judgement, they always identify me with the denominator that unites us: woman. And that is enough for our simple and authentic exchanges. The precision of their gestures, their way of moving, all of it is permeated with an involuntary elegance. I realize that my ignorance of their culture was a real plus, as it fostered discovery with all of my senses, without judgement, and with a beginner's thirst.

Once engulfed in this hodgepodge of mountains, it takes long weeks of intensive effort to get out. This day, I arrive at what will be my last village at this high altitude. It's the beginning of the afternoon. Before me is a small village which, for the occasion, is overflowing with life. I smile, observing from afar. I know this bustle; the presence of wooden, two-wheeled carts at the entrance of the village confirms it, it's market day! Woo-hoo! I speed up. The old ladies sell fresh cilantro, fresh onions, mandarin oranges, mountain potatoes, and lots of other things that I buy without knowing the name, but which have become familiar to me—like these spicy little seeds or fermented tofu. I slip into the market, I blend in. Here, no one looks at me strangely. I do as they do, bargain with the signs I've learned that represent the numbers one through ten. It's a holiday, I've never seen so many traditional costumes. I realize my great luck to be where I am today. My eyes fall on a small group of women set away from the crowd, with a young woman sitting in the back of a cart in the shade. Her incredible, shiny black hair almost touches the ground, and she looks like a princess. Meticulously, another woman gently untangles her hair. She's wearing beautiful red clothing. Is she preparing for her wedding? I continue on, I still need fresh garlic. I love the structures, the colors, the sounds of what we eat, like when we bite into a stalk of celery. Nourishing oneself is a three-dimensional experience. Even before buying my food, before harvesting or hunting, I go through a quick mental checklist: before, during, and after.

Before: where does my food come from and how was it cultivated? Is my food chemical-free? Did anyone have to kill a two-eyed creature for me to eat it?

During: how was it cooked? How am I going to cook it so that it keeps the maximum amount of its nutritional properties?

After: how much time and energy is my body going to use to digest this food? Often, I choose not to eat so as not to pollute my body with food that's "dead," by which I mean without life.

The sounds, the sensations, the colors—all of it is important when you're eating. And a stomach that's empty for long periods of time is going to want food at any price, not just to nourish it, but more important, to remove the unbearable feeling of hunger. And the hungrier you are, the more you see food in three dimensions. This is how I came to experience food at its root.

Over my twenty years of expeditions, I've pushed the adventure of hunger to the limit. Being hungry made me fantasize, hallucinate about food; in extreme situations I was even able to re-create smells, like that of bread coming out of the oven or even the scent of my mom's cherry omelettes. I could physically smell these odors in the air. It was simply the result of the work of my brain's imaging system. In the face of food deprivation, my brain created what my stomach desperately wanted!

Can you imagine the power we have within us? I'm not talking about physical power, but mental power. I live these extreme situations with such fascination for our being, body and spirit. Each of us has, at the base, a perfect machine, capable of so many things. Let's not limit ourselves! Let's go on an adventure to find the unexplored regions, right here, inside us—we, ourselves, are a destination of choice!

The crowd is so dense that I have to use my cart to elbow my way forward. Mules, water buffalo, and dogs also amble through. This whole population, each copper-colored face, transmits a calm and fluid energy. The sounds are natural, there's no frenetic honking, no aggressive slogans, as are usually spit out by loudspeakers in the roads of the Han provinces. At the far end of this little village, I find eggs. I'm so happy that I also buy myself a scalding hot tea that's served to me in a glass. The old lady smiles at me, she only has a few teeth left. She questions me and asks if I come from Nina. The sun is gentle, but at this altitude, the bottom note of the air is chilly. I watch the people move: the children are well-behaved, the dogs meander, always on the lookout for a bit of food. I haven't washed in weeks, my clothes are dirty, my hair is nothing but a mess of old sweat and dust. I haven't untangled it in weeks, and it's hidden beneath my warm hat. I go almost unnoticed in this crowd where the dust of the road covers more or less everything. I leave with a smile on my lips, following the only road that links the village to the outside world. I learned that it leads to Nina from talking to the woman who sold me my tea. Finally a name that's easy to pronounce! Naturally, Nina becomes my new destination.

Day by day, the valley floors widen, the trails are still made of dirt but my cart appreciates the surface, which betrays the numerous passings of vehicles. I can finally ask my way because I know my destination: I'm going to Nina. I'd gotten used to how precarious my life here is. I'm so glad I ventured into these mountains without knowing where I was going; I experienced a new form of letting go. It took balls of steel to venture into these mountains with neither maps nor GPS, without knowing the rules and regulations. I've come out with a rediscovered serenity, more intense, larger, more luminous. I found myself deprived of all points of reference, and I abandoned myself to these mountains, forgetting my greater mission. It was one day at a time, one step after the other. I had to stop, observe, let myself be guided. I took the risk; I wore the subtle perfume of permanent adventure.

Definition of adventure: "Any enterprise where the risk is considerable and the chances of success, dubious."

Nina, wait until I catch you . . .

From the day I arrive in Nina, I'm confronted by aggressive Hans. They accost me and demand to know whether I use a condom! A woman who's alone is considered to be a prostitute throughout the interior of China. The men with their crow-black, slick-backed hair look at me hard, then quietly turn away and observe me. I leave Nina after a good shower, sensing that I'm being observed. This feeling stays with me until the day I surprise a farmer working his field with a buffalo, who pulls out the very latest model digital camera to take a picture of me. Throughout my crossing of China, motorcyclists in black jackets come out of nowhere and take a photo of me with the same kind of camera. My days become psychologically trying. I hide, I sleep under bridges. Children throw stones at me each time I go through a village. It makes me sad, everything here is bereft of life energy. I discover cultures made in garbage, everything is polluted to the extreme. The earth is sucked dry, the water sources are open landfills. Chemical residues create a purplish-blue film on the water's surface. Agricultural plantations of all kinds are accelerated with the aid of nighttime lighting, tricking the plant's natural cycle so that it continues to grow at all hours. I'm in another world. Scenes from daily life break my heart. Animals are led alive to market for their meat. It's common to see fat, black goats, still alive, folded in two on a motorcycle, on either side of the luggage rack, held in place with cords that cut into their flesh. Roosters are suspended head-down on top of bags in the back. And just beneath the luggage rack, in a bag of rice, a dog cries out each time the driver goes over a bump, squashing him between the wheel and the rack. The list of cruelty toward animals goes on and on. Their cries of agony and despair still haunt me.

It throws me into a state of shock each time one of these vehicles passes me. This China has branded me forever; it's forced me to change my view of myself as a user of this planet. I'll never be the same. I've seen with my eyes, I've felt, I've cried before this human and animal misery.

The children are not children . . .

I'm relaxing under a tree set far back from the country road that I've just taken. Schoolchildren with big smiles observe me. There they are, joyful, and I'm happy to see them this way. They're not throwing rocks at me, for once. I start walking again, and they follow me, giggling, jumping around me. We talk a little, they're impressed by my cart. After a couple of miles, there are three children left, between six and eight years old. Night is gently falling, so I pick up the pace, but they follow my every step. I have to set up camp. So I go more than five hundred yards away from the road, well-hidden behind a big pile of gravel, the children still at my heels. I'm tired. I decide to sing while putting up my tent; this way the children can participate. I don't know what to do with these pairs of eyes stuck to me. They're happy, and very impressed by the tent. I'm careful to close up my cart. Just when I really start wondering about how odd it is to have these little sweethearts by my side now that it's almost dark, a charming little girl gives me a look from the corner of her eye. Her smile has disappeared and her eyes have narrowed. That seems strange. In the blink of an eye, she lifts the little black neoprene pocket that's attached to the right strap of my backpack and lays her hands on my BlackBerry phone. At the same moment, as though an invisible signal had chimed, the three of them scamper off into the night. I sit there openmouthed. Not only did they steal my precious phone, but they stabbed my heart, which thought that it had finally met children who were . . . children.

I silently rage to have trusted these kids. Then I smile in my anger; it's actually reassuring that after all my Chinese and Mongolian adventures, I'm still able to trust people. I go to bed without eating, without lighting my stove or my lamp. I just want to sleep. But first, I call Gregory in Switzerland on the satellite phone to let him know about the theft of my Black-Berry. He reminds me that I still have a second phone with a prepaid Chinese SIM card. I hang up, promising myself to be more careful in the future. I sink into my sleeping bag, where the whole world is better. Good night!

It's around midnight when two beams of light move across my tent. I wake up with a start. Voices approach. I open my tent, wearing my headlamp, which seems like a child's toy next to the powerful lights that are blinding me. I've quickly pulled on my Gore-Tex jacket and my hat. Two wiry men with skin weathered by the sun rush upon me, shouting in Mandarin. I don't understand anything; I gesture for them to sit down. They comply, the sound of the gravel crunching beneath their weight is reassuring to my ears. I wave away their huge, portable lamps with the back of my hand. I light my stove and make some tea. By the light of my stove, I can make out their faces. They look, or really, stare at me, openmouthed, as though they'd seen a rare endangered species, or a giraffe. I only have one cup, so I sacrifice two small, empty plastic bottles that I carry for unexpected situations. I cut well below the neck and serve a good, steaming cup of tea. It seems that the diplomatic approach is desirable in the present situation. I stay very calm. The tea is barely served when they start up again with their rapid-fire gibberish, accompanied by the occasional spray of spittle that lands on the flame of my stove. I explain to them that I don't understand; they shake their heads in despair. They seem to be saying, "She's really not very intelligent. Can't she even speak?" At this point, one of the two takes from his pocket a small, wrinkled paper with carefully drawn Chinese characters on it. I explain that I don't understand the written language, either. They raise their eyes skyward. I take the paper, and decide to tell them my story. I mime my misadventure with my cell phone when suddenly the quieter of the two men takes my BlackBerry out of his pocket and returns it to me. They both stand and disappear into the night, lamps extinguished. I sit there completely stupefied by the finality of their visit. I notice that they didn't touch their tea. I turn off my stove to be wholly engulfed in the night, it's more comforting for me. I'm so happy to have my phone back! I burrow into my sleeping bag, it's completely dark. A smile on my lips, I fall asleep.

At dawn, while breaking down my tent, I find the little paper with Chinese characters. I take a picture and send it to my contact in Beijing so he can translate it for me. A few minutes later, I get a text message translating it as follows: "We are teachers at the school and a student brought us a telephone that you lost." It's early, I hurry to get back on the road since I don't want to hang around here. After just ten minutes of walking, I run into the two gentlemen from the previous night, this time accompanied by their water buffalo, on their way to the fields. They are clearly not the village teachers. Their leathery skin had already given that away. I watch them step into their field. They don't greet me. All of this is very strange, nothing about it seems quite logical. Intrigued, I decide to examine it to see if it's still working. I have an access code and feel sure that there's no way they were able to use the phone—so I think. I go to the photo app, where I've saved a few cliché pics of mountain landscapes that I took in Mongolia as I hiked. I put the images on a slow slideshow, only to find that all the photos of China have been carefully erased, leaving only those of Mongolia. I can hardly believe it!

Shlurps and splashes

The sound of iron curtains being raised is part of the morning ritual. Entire families live in twenty-foot square rooms. The adults go outside and vigorously wash their heads with great splashes of water on the dirt path overlooking the road that passes for a sidewalk. There follows the long, interminable recital of expectoration, accompanied by the sounds required to make phlegm come up through the sinuses so it can be savored before being ingested. As a last recourse, they might blow their nose by blocking one nostril and pushing into the void as would a woman in the last phase of childbirth. What I'm saying here is that the Chinese are not germaphobes. One thing I observed in the interior provinces that I crossed is the Han's surprising use of phlegm. It's a bit like if you were to leave a Post-it note with your impressions of the food stuck to the wall. Here, you spit your best yellow loogie on to the wall. This means that the customers really liked the food and that they're honoring the cook.

Among the habits of these thousands of individuals, there's

a sound that I've baptized the "shlurp." It's made while they ingest their liquid foods, like the inescapable bouillon. There are so few crunchy things in their diet, like crackers, cookies, etc.; the consistency options range from liquid to soft to sticky. Feeding myself was an endless battle. I came to dream about eating the little, round, dehydrated disposable towelettes that I carry in the form of small, hard cakes. And for me, that's really saying something!

I'll spare you the steps that were necessary to obtain visas for my expedition, since they would fill a book on their own. At times, I was nostalgic for the gentle corruption of South America, where a fist with a bill discretely placed inside it was enough to cross borders. Or even long afternoons at the customs post in the mountains, waiting for the chief to deign to look at me a moment, before deciding to tell me his life story while sipping his favorite drink. It nearly always ended with a hug, the exchange of addresses and generous smiles, not to mention the necessary authorization accompanied by his blessings and the address of a family member whom I absolutely had to visit. It was a process that I learned to appreciate and cherish.

Well, China is a lot less fun, if I may say so, and very different from South America, where a person communicates their power in ways that range from the romantic to the dramatic. In China, you must save face above all else, which means keeping your face calm, immobile, with an expressionless gaze. Regardless of country or language, I've always succeeded at communicating with laughter, as in Mongolia when, after considerable effort, I was able to make the nomads laugh with mimed scenes from my journey, complete with sound effects. But here in China, what's most striking is the lack of flexibility: they don't understand my simplest mimed gestures. So I started thinking about it, and I came up with an idea having to do with Chinese characters. They don't represent one thing or movement, but a group of things, a scene. A Chinese character is a little like an entire situation, like if you were to take a picture. Perhaps because of this, they aren't able to isolate one gesture from a situation because that doesn't exist in their language.

The months of walking have passed without my being able to find or re-create the earlier magic of the mountains, with their different ethnic groups and their people dressed in flamboyant clothes with generous smiles. I've evolved in Han country. I've established very specific rules of survival so as to avoid problems, which can be summarized, for me as: white woman alone = avoid all people.

On this day, I move along a narrow mountain road, the miles slip by and I continue to follow this mountain slope. Below, there's the void, and if I look for the summit I see smooth, bare rock without flourishes, empty of any errant green growth that might accidentally have taken up residence. It's the end of the afternoon, and I'm looking for a place to put my tent. The ruts on either side of the road are chaperoned by bare rock to my right and empty space to my left. I'm going to have to walk until I find a little spot for my tent, and it's already dark. I won't turn on my headlamp, though. The moon is fairly high and its light will be just enough to help me avoid being seen.

A rivulet runs from the top of a gap that forms a "V" in the rock. A minuscule assemblage of two little rice paddies carpets the bottom. A dirt path the width of my tent leads to the rivulet. I decide to settle in here. I don't like it one bit, though, because I'm too close to the road. Tonight, I'll use my guylines, my tent has more than a dozen. Once these are taut, my tent looks like a spider with its legs stretched out. I attach the guylines, not with the goal of stabilizing the structure but with the idea of detecting any movement. These lines are the extension of my tent. If a human or animal approaches during the night, he won't see the cords and he'll get his feet caught in them, alerting me.

It's the hour when the night begins to retreat, the air seems pure again, and everyone is still sleeping, including me. Suddenly, my tent moves, a sharp jerk that awakens me; someone has been caught in my trap. I jump, put on my headlamp, and with practiced speed, open my tent. I discover a woman with deep wrinkles whose face has been burnished by time. Her grey hair is carefully pulled back and joined in a pretty bun low on her neck. I respectfully greet her in her language. She stops a moment, looks at me indifferently, and continues on her merry way toward the water. In the darkness, her gaze is now attentive to the ground. She's carrying on her right shoulder a pitchfork that seems heavy for her frail silhouette. She stops at the creek and, with a rapid movement of her hand, collects water, brings it to her lips, then crosses from one terrace to the next with the aid of the big rock placed on the ground in front of the first rise.

I return to my tent to sleep, there is no danger. Ideally, I'd like to sleep for another hour. I sink back into my sleeping bag with delectation and fall asleep immediately. I escape in a series of dreams where I'm swimming, but really it's all muddled— until the moment I wake up. I give a yelp of fear: objects are floating all around the tent and my sleeping bag is under water. Everything is flooded. I don't understand. I jump out of my tent to see what's going on, and one glance is enough! Ah, the vengeful old crone!

Small canals are constructed throughout the terraced rice plantation to redirect the water. And just above my tent is a tiny one, hastily built with claylike earth. The old lady blocked the creek at an intersection upstream, forcing the creek into the canals, including the one above my tent. Then she carefully dug the canal level with the entrance of my tent, causing this flooding. I can't believe it, I'm now going to have to spend several nights in this wet sleeping bag. It's not warm enough for my gear to dry. I stand barefoot in front of my tent, shaking it in the face of this willful sabotage. At that moment, silently and with an imperceptible smile at the corners of her mouth, the old lady passes in front of my tent and slips away into the early hours of a day that's already proven to be frustrating.

It will take me more than ten days to dry my sleeping bag and the rest of my things, since the temperature is 50°F with highs between 62 and 68°. I decide to push into the mountains, as far as possible from these people. I look at my self-proclaimed "tourist" maps and notice an annotation in an isolated zone. It reads "Panda Reserve." This discovery gives me new energy; I'll head toward the panda reserve. What is a panda reserve, anyway? I don't have any idea, but it's to the north, and that's the right direction. Off I go. . . .

With this motivation, I start to gain altitude, pulling my cart along muddy paths. The effort is tiresome. Everything hurts.

I sleep in the only dry clothes I have left, then I put on my pants and my Gore-Tex jacket. I delicately place my wet sleeping bag over me, for the insulation. At night, it's only just above freezing. It feels like the humidity is penetrating my body. I get little sleep; my muscles and bones don't like that, my whole skeleton hurts. I just keep moving deeper into these mountains. I want only to be surrounded by Mother Nature, to not have to worry about anything but my own world.

The days pass, the villages become more sparse. I passed through the last one four days ago; I continue to climb. I'm now at eight thousand feet. Around me a pine forest smiles. It's airy with beautiful clearings. I lay all my gear out on the ground and decide to take advantage of the sun and comfort that this beautiful forest offers me. It's my first comforting situation since the flood. I put up my tent. There's no humidity here, the ground is covered with a thick layer of dry pine needles that pleasantly insulates me and emits this scent that I love. For the first time since the old lady flooded me, I feel good. I make use of the sun and arrange all of my wet belongings on the ground, including my sleeping bag. I take off the clothes I'm wearing, only keeping on the first layer, the sun is so warm. I position myself to soak up the most heat possible. I need to get rid of all this dampness that's in my body. I'm constantly cold. But today is a magnificent day. . . . *Thank you, thank you . . .*

I carefully turn over my gear, hoping that at the end of the day everything will be dry. Meanwhile, I decide to completely take apart my stove for some thorough maintenance. I've used so much blended fuel that everything is clogged up, and despite the pressure, the burner only gives off a small flame and sputters. I take out my repair kit and, carefully, I take it apart piece by piece. Everything is covered with a velvety black soot. Deliberately, I place all the parts on a plastic bag, giving particular attention to their original placement. Hours later, I'm still sitting in the same position in front of my tent. My hands are black and it's all over my face, too, but I'm smiling. I just lit my MSR fuel stove and it's purring like the day I bought it. I jump for joy, I did it! That night, I sleep like a baby inside my sleeping bag. The day's sun has given the Michelin man back his curves. It's acted as a balm on my body.

The days pass without my being able to recall the Tuesday that it supposedly is, and even less, the month. And yet, I'm able to wake up each morning and be enthralled by the day that greets me. I accept it as a single, unique day, where each little detail makes the ensemble of my days extraordinary. One morning, even before opening the vestibule of my tent, I can feel that today is different. Outside, everything is covered in a coat of white. The smells have changed, the air is purified, sharp. I don't like routine, so I happily accept the snow's invitation. At this altitude, everything changes quickly.

The ground is carpeted with mud blended with snow, the different densities of the structures make me smile. The snow, with its airy structure, looks remarkably like stiff egg whites, which transports me in the blink of an eye to my mom's kitchen, where I made my first sponge cakes and meringues. I haven't seen a soul since I entered the so-called Panda Reserve. I haven't seen any informational signs advising me of my entry. I advance, sweating big drops, pushing, pulling my cart on the only county road that rises to ten thousand feet. Here, the bamboo rhizome has secretly worked underground and has cordoned off every possible inch of ground, like a silent invasion. I'm now just a few steps from the summit. If I look at the valley floor, I see a dense swath of bamboo bathed in a milky fog. I realize that the bamboo has choked off any possibility of another species flourishing in this soil. To me, it seems like an invader. I've gotten cold since stopping, so I put on my jacket and take out my dented little Thermos. I filled it this morning with good black tea and lemon.

To escape the mud, I spot a large rock above a culvert that passes under the road. I put my things down on the roadside and sit down on the rock. I enjoy my tea, and just sit for a moment, imagining that what I'm looking at could potentially be panda habitat. In Mandarin, this animal is called "bear-cat." It eats as much as forty-five pounds of bamboo per day. Dreamily, I scan the mountains while sipping my tea, with the same pleasure a smoker takes in the day's first cigarette. My beverage is still hot, and for the hiker it represents extra motivation in this terrain that's so empty of reward. During the night, the temperature at this altitude went down to well below freezing. My hat is pulled down over my head, but my ears are intentionally left out in the air. The atmosphere is freezing, foggy, but astonishingly silent. Suddenly a fine and almost imperceptible melody seems to float on the air. It sounds like a handful of sharp notes tumbling together. The melody seems strangely fragile. I look for its source, without success, so I use the moment to swallow another sip of tea. At that moment, an isolated breeze comes up from the valley, causing the melody to ring out just behind me, this time brighter and clearer. I turn around and notice that the bamboo leaves above the path are as white as porcelain. They're frozen through. The gust from the bottom of the valley reached the leaves which, in knocking against each other, create this plaintively resonant, but elegant melody.

A warmth rises within me and stirs my senses and my whole being. I just received one of the numerous lessons that Mother Nature has taught me. I'm thankful and, eyes closed, I listen with my heart to the lament of the bamboo.

My teacup is still in my hands. After a long moment of stillness, I open my eyes. I'm serene, nature is speaking to me again. I've missed it so much in all the hustle and bustle of China. There I am, motionless on my rock, when I see something stirring down below in the dried-up creek passing under the road. Suddenly a little ball, dark reddish-brown in color, rushes forward, exposed and defenseless, for a hundred yards in the creek bed. It's just enough to let me get a look at its little body and its long striped tail. I'm left dumbstruck. I've just seen a very rare animal: a red panda, *Ailurus fulgens*.

The same day, a military convoy of several all-terrain vehicles passes me in the panda reserve. The next day, at the day's end, five special agents with identification badges around their necks stop me in a bamboo forest where I've set up camp for the night. I finally understand why they're shouting at me like that; they were certain they would catch me making a fire! To their great surprise, they discover a contraption that makes flames but doesn't use wood: my stove. None of the officials speak a word of English, but their city clothes tell me that they've come from far away. I do a demonstration and put my teapot on to boil. They leave, tail between their legs, really quite disappointed. I watch them walk down to the road, and call after them, "You're not staying for tea?" It's cold, the fog is dense, everything is soggy. I haven't been through a village in a week, how were they able to find me so precisely in this forest? I think I'd rather not know. I keep my guard up, but that won't be enough.

It happens two valleys later, on a morning like any other, grey and rainy, while I'm walking up a road to the north, along the stream near the border. It's there that my friends the Chinese put a definitive end to my progress. Appearing suddenly, they encircle me with unmarked black cars, a kind I've seen many times before. They're all wearing the same black leather jacket. I can't believe it, I feel like I'm in an old James Bond movie. A young rookie stands twenty inches from my face screaming the word "passport." The scene that follows is more of the same with these guys running in all directions, carrying information to two apparently key characters who hold themselves apart. I don't know who these people are. Then the army arrives. I decide not to look anyone in the eye so as not to provoke them. When they speak to me, I don't understand anything, but I don't make any effort, either. I just shrug my shoulders uncomprehendingly. It goes on for hours. At the beginning of the intervention, the young rookie confiscated the BlackBerry that was in the front pocket attached to my backpack. He didn't see that I had another with a Swiss SIM card. From the inside of my pocket, I send a blind message to Switzerland: "Stopped by the Chinese police." There reigns an intense agitation and it's definitely not because of me. No, they must be concerned about something else. This perception is primordial for me. I wait in the background without anyone interacting with me or explaining what's going on. After several hours, I get up to get my Thermos out of my cart. At this moment, the older of the two chiefs steps in front of me, gesturing with indescribable arrogance. He motions for me to get into the car. And for the first time, I say no! With one delicate but sharp movement, I snatch my passport from his hands, an action which completely disconcerts him, but he doesn't show it, as his culture demands. I bend down slowly and put on my backpack, take my cart, and retrace my steps back from where I came—as slowly as I'm able, with no sudden movements, and without looking at anyone. I'm expecting them to run after me, or worse. But nothing! I can't believe it!

I decide to return to the last village I crossed, about a mile away. I certainly don't want them to be able to charge me with fleeing the law. I'll wait in the village. And if they want to arrest me, I'll be there. Next, I call my embassy in Beijing with which I established a relationship as I prepared for my expedition. Then I call Switzerland, to explain my situation. At the village, I get the news of my expulsion: I have five days to leave the country. Will it be enough? I'm in the west of China, right against the Himalayan range. And so begins a race against the clock. My expedition leader immediately alerts my contact in Beijing to organize the fastest possible transfer. I'll leave from the nearest airport, which is in Jiuzhai Huanglong. In order to build landing strips long enough to allow a big Boeing to serve the famous Jiuzhaigou National Park, they razed the top of a mountain! I can't believe it. I return via Chengdu, then Beijing. As soon as I arrive, I go to the Swiss embassy to let them know I'm alright. Meanwhile, Gregory and my Beijing contact have prepared the papers I need so that I can go directly to the Mongolian embassy and get a visa. The timing is extremely tight. While I'm in line in front of the Mongolian embassy, my plane ticket is in the process of being electronically issued. My turn arrives at the exact moment my BlackBerry tells me that an e-mail has arrived in my in-box. This e-mail contains the ticket that I must have in order to obtain my visa. The next day, completely exhausted by the events of the last few days, I board a flight from Beijing to Ulaanbaator.

I'll later learn that my arrest was preventive. Exactly twelve miles away, the same morning I was walking up that damp road, a young monk self-immolated in a temple. That day, out of nowhere, police forced tourists arriving from the other direction off the local bus. I assume that the authorities didn't want a Westerner to be able to report the incident. Monks have been setting themselves on fire for years as a sign of protest against the regime's oppression.

7. Gobi Desert—Third Attempt

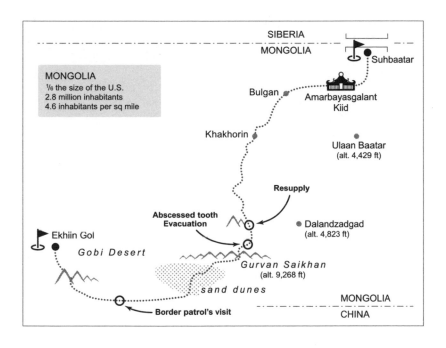

SIBERIA

MONGOLIA

Suhbaatar

MONGOLIA
⅛ the size of the U.S.
2.8 million inhabitants
4.6 inhabitants per sq mile

Bulgan

Amarbayasgalant
Kiid

Khakhorin

Ulaan Baatar
(alt. 4,429 ft)

Resupply

**Abscessed tooth
Evacuation**

Dalandzadgad
(alt. 4,823 ft)

Ekhiin Gol

Gobi Desert

Gurvan Saikhan
(alt. 9,268 ft)

sand dunes

MONGOLIA

Border patrol's visit

CHINA

Early May 2011—I set out once again

I'M FINALLY READY TO LEAVE. BECAUSE WINTER WAS blowing its worst, I did what I could before I left to amass gear designed for extreme cold weather, but the blizzard was so violent that even my tent, conceived for the base camp of Everest, wasn't holding up.

I'm back in the tourist camp, not far from my GPS departure point. I'll be able to get back there tomorrow at dawn. Damn it! This Gobi Desert hasn't been an easy one.

I find the same Mongolian girls still working there. Degi welcomes me with open arms, like an old friend passing through. She brings me into the main yurt and orders tea. Despite her little polo shirt and baseball cap, Degi carries within her all the hospitality of the generations of Mongolian women who preceded her.

The mistress of the house is obliged to receive guests, but it doesn't stop there. At the moment of your departure, she will accompany you over the first few hundred yards, as if to share with you the first steps of your new road and give you strength for your journey. In these parts, it's better to travel in twos. Survival in this sparsely populated country depends on hospitality. (With only 4.6 inhabitants per square mile, it's the least inhabited country on the planet.)

Degi, with a precise gesture of her right hand, invites me to sit down. It seems insignificant, but I've seen this gesture countless times during my Mongolian adventures. Hospitality in this country manifests itself in exact gestures, passed from mother to daughter, and it's no different with Degi. Sitting before a steaming cup of tea, she tells me the latest news from her corner of the Gobi. She's very happy to see me and impatient to know the outcome of my adventures. We start in on a conversation that will last several hours. "Let's start from the beginning," she exclaims, "what happened after your second attempt in the middle of winter? Do you know that we're still talking about it here? Where did you go?" (In the middle of this, the camp's cook sticks her head in the door and nods sympathetically. I think I must be her worst nightmare, a vegetarian!)

Amid the so-called high-priority news, I learn that I just missed the actor Richard Gere, who stayed here with his team. They came to scout for a future film telling the story of the Dalai Lama's life. Degi doesn't know anything more, but she's eager to show me the photo of the group taken in the company of "Sir Richard Gere," as she calls him. I have fun with it and she starts to do the same. "You know that I *will* get over my disappointment at not having seen him?"

"I'm not so sure!" she responds, looking at me mischievously. We burst into girlish giggles. It does me good to find a little feminine camaraderie. During our talks, we cover travel, the practice of yoga, the complexity of being a vegetarian in Mongolia, and of course, the question of men. Degi's English is very good, and I take perhaps too much advantage of it; it's so rare for me to be able to go beyond the habitual questions, "How old are you? Where is your husband?"

Degi always responds with great patience to my most serious and insistent questions about Mongolia, its politics, and all that's implicit in the numerous cultural codes of this country. She tries her best to shed light on my innumerable challenges with her people. In a way, she becomes my cultural counselor with whom I leave my most sensitive files.

I tell her about the ghost incident. It happened a couple of hundred miles north of here. The wind was blowing as usual, and up from the sandy earth blew clouds that appreciably reduced visibility. A vehicle came out of nowhere and didn't see me until the last minute. My clothes were the color of sand, and dirty. I was wearing a patched scarf to protect my head. The vehicle slowed down, pulled up next to me, and suddenly I saw a large man who was absolutely horrified. He rolled up his window quick as lightning, emitting little screams and jumping in his seat as though his nether regions were on fire. In despair, he pressed his foot down on the accelerator before finally melting into the cloud of sand.

Degi easily decodes the meaning of this situation. "You know, there's a legend," she tells me, "that warns the traveler about meeting the wrong kind of person. She's symbolized by a wandering white woman traveling on foot, who is none other than a ghost of ill omen."

The following dawn, the sweet music of my gaiters' friction against each other once again flutters in my ears. I go southward, toward a mini saddle that will give me access to the Gobi Gurvan Saikhan National Park.

As soon as I climb up to the pass, I'm thrilled to be back here. The temperature has fallen drastically, the wind is destabilizing as usual, no matter what moment of the day. The landscape is lunar, bare, hard sand dunes whose color varies between dirty grey and light brown. I get into the habit of waiting until noon to take a break, since that's when it's warmest.

That day, I'm in the middle of setting up my stove when I sense something moving far away. I get up, but can't make anything out. I go back to my stove when, out of the corner of my eye, I see movement. I grab my small binoculars. I don't have to wait long before I find it in my sights. I smile, what beauty! It's a wolf. He observes me, but in his way he knows that he shouldn't stay too long out in the open. So he plays at examining me, sniffing me, then he pulls back and moves away, goes to take cover, then reappears farther away. This little game of hide-and seek charms me. The animal still has his winter coat, a magnificent mouse grey, that he's in the process of losing.

I go down into the interior of this plateau at an altitude where Gobi goats come to see me. I'm surprised by the temperature, which has dangerously plummeted. At dawn, as soon as I wake up, I sense something abnormal in the air. In front of my tent, the water in the creek has frozen. I get up and am euphoric at the incredible scene before me. The mountains are white, powdered with snow, which contrasts with the ground, which wasn't visited by the flakes. I stop, I film, I take photos. This landscape is magnificent. For miles around, there's nothing. But the wind rises and gets bad. That night, I look a long time for a depression in the terrain. I put on my ski goggles to save my eyes, which have already suffered enough from the sun and wind.

The days pass, but the wind doesn't calm down one bit. One day, while hiding behind a big hill of dirt, a large dog comes up to me. We take a liking to each other, I give him massages. His coat is adapted to this climate, he's like a big, long-haired teddy bear. Suddenly, a motorcycle appears at the back of a hollow. The driver stops and takes off his traditional coat. His ventral belt holds in a big, round belly. Without a word, he stretches out on the ground in front of me and starts playing with some small stones in his left hand. Then he raises his head; he's wearing a faded baseball cap and a sort of mouth cover, attached behind his ears, in front of his mouth. The bit of cloth looks strangely like what Scheherazade wore in the tale of *"One Hundred and One Nights."* I laugh silently, the image of this fat nomad lying at my feet with his face scarf is too surreal . . . until he starts coughing, and coughing, and coughing. I then understand the protective function of his mask: tuberculosis, as well as good old meningitis, and other infectious diseases are still at large in this part of the world. After his coughing fit, he mimes and I understand clearly that he's proposing to keep me warm during the night. And then he smiles! Wow . . . and continues to shyly throw little rocks here and there. Ah! These Mongolians, they're unstoppable! I hurriedly drag out my fake husband, and with an outraged and very serious air, I explain that I'm married. After a good hour, he gets up, this time with considerably less panache, and leaves without a word, coughing away on his motorcycle. I almost feel sorry for him.

The next day, he reappears on the horizon. My four-legged companion is still with me. Without speaking, the man slowly passes in front of me and throws a bit of meat to the dog to lure him away. The dog sniffs the morsel and follows the trail of the exquisite odor given off by the meat that the man places at regular intervals to bring the dog back with him. It turns out that it's his dog.

Water sources are rare and hidden. I have to look for them. Those that are marked on my old maps have probably dried out by now, or are otherwise nonexistent or even salty. I'm forced to zigzag to find water. The wells are level with the ground, you have to have a good eye to spot them. In places, they're protected by an animal skin, which is then covered by a large rock. All this zigzagging isn't great when you're trying to cover miles, but it allows me to discover unique and removed places where I surprise gazelles, bighorn sheep, and even ibex. It's almost a treasure hunt, where water, "blue gold," is the ultimate reward. I search, I excavate, I crisscross this desert, I climb rock formations to see into the distance from their summit. During my hunt for water, I stumble upon magnificent petroglyphs showing scenes of a snow leopard hunt. I camp in a forest of saxauls, the only trees capable of surviving in the Gobi. I'm later told that it's populated with wolves . . . and to think that I slept there like a baby! On the other hand, that same night I met a splendid lizard, good-sized, with lemon-yellow feet, as well as Bar-

bary ground squirrels, which communicate through high-pitched little cries. Balanced on their two hind legs, they sniff the air in nervous little jolts to learn of imminent danger. I'm amazed by the fauna and flora of this desert. It must be said that I'm wildly lucky to have come here on foot. I expend considerable energy and a lot of sweat to cross these endless sandy hollows, only to have before me yet another of these plains that looks like an obstacle course. It's during this period that the end-of-day storms start. With the wind, the cold, and the rationing of food and water, the conditions are perfect for a drastic loss of weight and a weakening of my body. . . .

In places, the ground is covered with purple and pink flowers and even wild irises. Each day has its beauty, its discovery.

Two-humped camels that locals call "the vessels of the desert" move about in the scenery. I've observed them for days. I've understood that when the end-of-day storm explodes (and believe me, it's not a small storm), the camels all leave together in a single direction that's always the right one. So I keep an eye on them and do the same. They're the best meteorologists I've met.

I've hardly seen anyone since I left my resupply point six miles ago. Food is scarce, and my zigzags to find water are wearing me out. I'm walking with nothing but a cup of muesli soaked in water for breakfast and a handful of rice or lentils for dinner. That night, the temperature drops to -5°F and my body experiences the beginnings of hypothermia from the lack of food, warmth, and water. The tourist camp is now only twenty-five miles away, the people there are expecting my arrival, and I'm late. Since they had gone out to pick up personnel and food for the camp, they logically came looking for me on their way back. They find me. I'm weak and trembling, but still walking.

I accept the invitation of the camp's director who promises that she'll drop me back off at the same spot once I've recuperated and had a good shower.

I shiver all night long, and the people there do shifts to bring me big Thermoses of hot water. Meanwhile, Gregory, who is meeting me, looks in vain for the tourist camp which is just a cluster of yurts in the middle of the desert. An error in entering the GPS coordinates leaves him alone, despairing, looking at his Mongolian driver who's decided to sleep for a bit. They arrive at the camp the next day at dawn. They were less than forty miles away. They find me thin and run-down. We laugh about his little misadventure—I've always said that a GPS without a good topo map is useless!

The next day, I decide to wash my hair in the sunshine, in front of my yurt. I fill two old plastic bottles with well water. I let down my hair, which is in a state close to a bird's nest and, blindly, grab a bottle and empty it over my head. Suddenly, a very generous expletive escapes my mouth, followed by "I can't believe it!" Alerted by my exclamations, Gregory hurries over to find that I just emptied my spare fuel, which was in a similar plastic bottle. I think it takes him a good half hour to stop laughing.

The strong smell stays with me for days. . . .

A Kindle without words . . .

What I really miss the most are books. They're much too heavy for me to carry, though occasionally I'll bring one or two books that I religiously savor. Then, sadly, I end up burning the pages.

I thought I'd found the solution by ordering, via satellite phone, a present for my thirty-ninth birthday: a Kindle, an e-book reader. I immediately gave my expedition leader the titles I dreamed of reading, new books as well as classics to reread. He confirmed more than once that all was well and that he'd take care of the Kindle situation.

So, with assured enthusiasm, I ask Gregory for my present.

I'm so excited to finally get to read that I quickly unwrap the package and turn it on. I don't yet dare to fully believe it: I hold in my hands dozens of books, enclosed in a little tablet no bigger than two chocolate bars. I start to navigate the menu, I find an integrated dictionary, and . . . and . . . I look everywhere, but there's nothing else. I turn to my expedition chief—I must have an expression of total desolation on my face—and demand, "Where are the books?"

He looks at me briefly, making himself look very busy, and says something like, "You asked for a Kindle, and I brought you a Kindle, right? And you're going to take it with you, because I sure won't be bringing it back with me."

That is how I came to take my Kindle on a little tour of the Gobi Desert. Did I already mention it didn't contain a single book?

Several weeks later, I report to my expedition chief, via text messages, the unfortunate adventure of Mr. Kindle. Due to the effects of extreme temperatures and despite my precautions, my Kindle, my beautiful Kindle is transformed into a home-made pancake: it melts!

I'm not sure that said Kindle was tested for dry, windy zones, or temperatures reaching 110°F or more.

Alright, fine, I've got it. Each time I've tried to improve my nomadic existence, it hasn't worked. I'm just going to continue with things as they are. Without books, without anything . . .

I don't yet know that it will go on for three years.

Nice, warm feet

I take off again with good clothes, a huge, warm sleeping bag, and my cart full of good food. (I listened to the advice of Mongolians about the possible temperatures this time of year in the mountains of the Gobi.)

I cross the singing dunes, which are a thousand feet high and where the sand rubs against the wind and vibrates, producing a roar that's like an airplane taking off right over your head. It's truly an extraordinary phenomenon. It takes me five days to cross them. I pull my cart, which sinks into the sand without my even moving it. In my herculean effort, I get to see a herd of camels trotting across the dunes. As for the sandstorms that come up at the end of the day, they're clearly less fun!

On the other side of the dunes I find firm ground where my cart seems to fly. From that point on, I have a magnificent adventure, hard but full of pure and beautiful discoveries. I scale some rocks to discover the biggest nest I've ever seen, a vulture's nest. I run into Chinese geologists in the process of core sampling, in my opinion, illicitly! I zigzag again and again across this Gobi that's heating up slowly as I move deeper into it.

I leave behind the last Gobi village, Gurvantes, and plunge even deeper into the desert, heading west. I'm not far from the Chinese border when I run into some yurts with big solar panels. It's none other than the research center dedicated to snow leopards.[4] The scientists welcome me with great respect; they can well imagine the effort it took to arrive here. They live in this camp for up to three months at a time and trek through the surrounding mountains to plant cameras, among other things, that allow them to take precise censuses, as well as to take stock of the local population. It's painstaking work with lots of effort over many years that's starting to bear fruit. I'm lucky enough to spend an entire day with a researcher, placing cameras . . . and guess what we did? We spent the day walking, of course! Months later, once they've recovered the cameras, I receive a photo taken by one of them. A heartfelt thanks to these scientists for giving me this rare opportunity.

Farther on, I'm stopped by border guards who, after thirty long minutes, succeeded at tracking me to my camp, which I'd decided to set up in the rocks. With them is the horrible Mongolian who must be from the Altai Mountains, and not from this region. I ran into him days ago, his unusually dark skin made him stand out and his rabbit-killer eyes made him impossible for me to forget, the little fink. He informed on me in the hope of getting money or of having the border guards in his pocket. Who knows? There's all kinds of trafficking here, close to the border and far from prying eyes.

I come out of it well enough, after a nice little chat and a cup of tea. One of the guards slips me his e-mail address in case of "problems." I thank them for the visit and look the rabbit killer straight in the eyes before he leaves. They're the last humans I'll meet and also the wildest part of my expedition

---

4. www.snowleopard.org

before reaching Ekhiin Gol. This crossing will leave me with a precise taste of what the body secretes when it constantly needs water. The temperature stays at 122°F for days. With no possible shelter, I can only wait for the right moment beneath my makeshift tarp, the moment when the sun will allow me to advance without becoming dehydrated. I make an unforgettable crossing, bathed in this madness-inducing wind. This desert that refused me twice before will accept my steps the third time.

And so I arrive from the east, where there's no path, beneath the stupefied gaze of the few inhabitants of this community isolated from everything, Ekhiin Gol.

8. Siberia

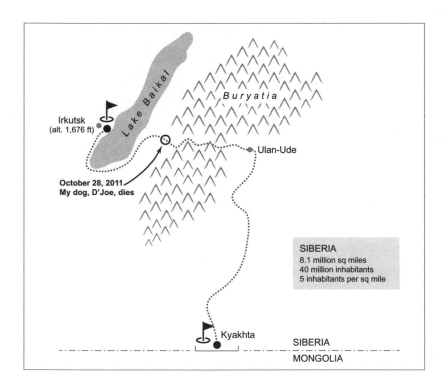

Irkutsk
(alt. 1,676 ft)

Lake Baikal

Buryatia

Ulan-Ude

October 28, 2011
My dog, D'Joe, dies

SIBERIA
8.1 million sq miles
40 million inhabitants
5 inhabitants per sq mile

Kyakhta

SIBERIA
MONGOLIA

My second passport just arrived with a three-month Russian visa! Wow! This time, my application was accepted, I just had to explain what kind of conferences I give throughout the world and the subjects I discuss. I'm super happy.

The next day, at night, my plane lands at the Irkutsk airport in Siberia. Natalia, my local contact who's helped me with the preparations, waits for me a bit, while inside the customs zone a tall Russian in a bottle-green uniform is performing my baggage inspection with particular zeal. She explains that I'll need to pay an additional fee for overweight baggage. The exorbitant sum that I already paid in Mongolia doesn't concern her. "Here, Russia!" she says.

Her voice has exactly the tone that you would imagine. The official looks me straight in the eye and for the first time I hear the phrase, "It's procedure." Her tone leaves little hope, but despite the lateness of the hour (one o'clock in the morning), I expend a little energy. I firmly intend not to let myself be had by an official in need of some cash, so I decide to call her on her little game. I start to take out all my gear, right there on the floor, in the middle of the walkway, spreading my stuff out as much as possible: cart, cooking pot, water pump, tent, camping mattress, etc.

A hollow but amused laugh rings out. "And why didn't you bring your husband with you?" Squatting, I lift my head and respond with exactly the type of answer she wants to hear: "Well, he has to work a little, doesn't he?"

In a burst of laughter, she motions for me to collect my strange belongings and go. This is how I officially enter Siberia.

August 1, 2011, Port Baikal

I'm on the shores of Lake Baikal, which I'm looking at for the first time. Its tranquil power impresses me. According to the basic maps I was able to find at Irkutsk, I'm going to be able to make my way around the south end of the lake. But from my first steps, I'm stuck between the lake and the rocks. I walk (or really, jump) for more than seven days following the railroad track, the only space available. My cart, which normally trails behind me without too much difficulty, is attached to my belt by two large carabiners. Using this method, I go through 39 tunnels and cross 248 bridges. (Looking back, I smile; I can still see myself with my headlamp at the entrance to a tunnel, listening to see if a train is approaching before plunging, head lowered, into this black and humid pit.) What really worries me are the many types of trains that run on this line: homemade carts that the locals ride in between official trains, groups of tourists crammed into old-fashioned wagons pulled by an ancient steam engine, and the official train that serves as a shuttle at supposedly regular hours.

Nature takes the upper hand when she can and imposes herself majestically. Wildflowers are everywhere, tall and elegant, dense and intense in their shades. The light air exhales scents of humus and chlorophyll. Below, on the near side of the cliffs, the hypnotic Mr. Baikal displays himself for admiration. Far away, freshwater Baikal seals timidly emerge with their little round heads, shimmering black. They stay just long enough to catch their breath and disappear, leaving the water undisturbed. Baikal seals (*Pusa sibirica*) are among the very few species of freshwater seal in the world. There are sixty thousand of them in Lake Baikal.

Now as I sit along the shores of this great lake, my fishing rod is at rest, as the edge of the lake is inhabited by otters and seals. I don't want to risk accidentally catching one of these magnificent inhabitants of the bank so, for the moment, I abstain.

I start off on the wrong foot . . .

Upon my arrival in Slyudyanka, I discover another reality bathed in poverty and the pollution that the cellulose factory[5] leaves behind. Covert glances, furtive silhouettes coming out of the forest, faces weathered by alcohol, faded eyes emptied of light. Men

---

5. This factory shut its doors at the end of 2013.

hang around here and there, they seem like they're waiting. Hope abandoned this part of the world long ago. They call the people here, "The ones the government forgot."

It's too late to keep going, so I'll have to sleep here. Unfortunately, the basic hotels that I find don't want to take me and physically push me out, yelling at me. I go all over town without success. Either they tell me they're full, or they don't want me. So I call Natalia, who's outraged by the situation and by the dubious schemes against me. She warns me: something smells rotten. "I'll make a few calls and then call you back," she adds.

Not long after, she announces that she's found a place where I'll be able to sleep in safety, but it's at the other end of town.

She's worried, as her sources have told her that my arrival created quite a commotion and that there would be some guys waiting on the road to rob me. She asks me to wait so she can think about the next step. I hang up a little perplexed. The telephone rings again. "OK, I have family in the village after Slyudyanka. They're coming to get you. And they'll drop you back off at the village. Make sure you tell everyone that friends of mine are coming to get you, don't say where you're going, it's imperative."

After this close call, I pass through towns—no matter how small—stopping only at the small general store to resupply. Then I plunge like a wild animal into the forest, where I'm safe.

Birch and spruce share the terrain with flies, mosquitos, and other unidentified flying specimens that pursue me in clouds. The intensity that the taiga forest exudes is palpable and in total contradiction with the inhabitants of this region of the world.

The south of Siberia seems to be decomposing like a mushroom in slow motion. There reigns an energy that devours those who haven't understood that each instant is survival. The cubic carcasses of every kind of concrete from the Soviet era are still here and there, naked like skeletons.

The taiga is spellbinding and magnificent, I love this dense and vibrant forest. In this season, it's bursting with berries: raspberries, blueberries, and a multitude of kinds I've never seen. I feast on those I know. I live in the taiga, showing myself only rarely. Even in the wilderness I stay hidden; bears also feed on blueberries. During all this time, I can't even pee without clouds of starving mosquitos having a feeding frenzy on my buttocks. But I love this wild and extreme side of the forest. The cold and the rain, with a ray of sunshine here and there, enliven my days.

My D'Joe . . .

Lying in my tent, I get a text message via my satellite phone that says "Call me back quickly. Subject: D'Joe." I pick up my cell phone, angry with myself for leaving it off for too long. I'm able to reach my mom, who's taking care of my dog in my absence. She tells me the bad news: "D'Joe's health has suddenly gone downhill."

I immediately fall apart. I knew this might happen. But between the understanding of the head and the heart, there's a discrepancy that I'm living out now. I talk to him as I've always done, but the satellite phone changes the voice. I ask my mom to remember to cook him his favorite pasta and I hang up.

I can't stop crying, alone in my tent in the middle of this thick forest that I suddenly find oppressive. Nothing in the world could console me. Night comes and I spend it sobbing. Then at dawn, eyes swollen, heart empty, with nothing left, I suddenly smell a familiar scent engulfing my tent. Almost imperceptible at first, then very strong: it's the soft odor of my dog, particular, sweet, and elegant all at once, and at the same time refined. I sit there, shocked, in the morning light.

Less than a week later, he dies.

I cross Siberia under the weight of grief. Not a day passes that I don't think of him, even today.

Sitting on the side of a dirt road, I take off my gloves and get out my Thermos, which is carefully placed in a lateral pocket of my backpack. A noise catches my attention, and I lift my head. An innate protective reaction causes me to jump backward just in time as a dozen army tanks hurtle past at full throttle. I'm just a few miles from the Mongolian border, and military vehicles and uniforms of all kinds roam the terrain like ants.

At the bottom of a long descent, Kyakhta suddenly appears. A border town of about ten thousand people, it was rich and opulent in the days when Siberian furs passed through on their way south, and tea came through by caravan from China. I'm curious to see what's left of it today. I let the small, wooden houses surrounded by decrepit fences parade by; corrugated metal and rust serve as decoration. The faces are closed. I've arrived, Mongolia is just a mile or two away.

I find myself an instant coffee to drink, leaning on a mini counter. Passersby look at me dumbstruck, but without further curiosity. That's exactly what it is, "without further curiosity."

There is nothing different here. And yet I imagine the caravans of old times, the dust rising with their passage, the sounds, the strong smells of animal excrement in the road, the laughs of the merchants, the shouting matches at street corners, the comings and goings.

I lift my head; for a moment I'd lost myself in the warm steam of my coffee. A cold wind blows across my bones. The background of forest, which stands seemingly ready to eat the city, is now mottled with splotches of golden yellow, brilliant red, and all the magnificent shades of autumn. Winter isn't far off.

Mission accomplished, Siberia is behind me.

EXplorAsia continued: I'll go back to Irkutsk from where my plane will take me to Bangkok, where my resupply is. From there, I'll have to go to Boten, in the very north of Laos at the Chinese border, where I'll finally be able to get back to my expedition's original route all the way to Australia.

9. Laos

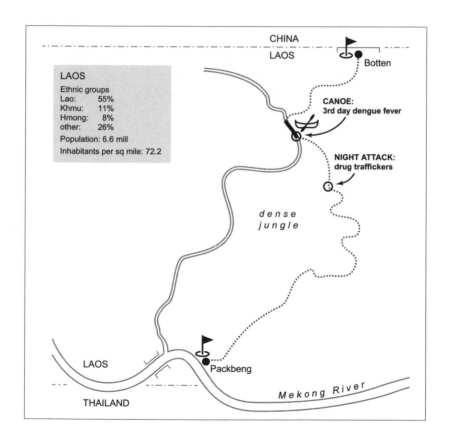

CHINA
LAOS
Botten

LAOS
Ethnic groups
Lao: 55%
Khmu: 11%
Hmong: 8%
other: 26%
Population: 6.6 mill
Inhabitants per sq mile: 72.2

CANOE:
3rd day dengue fever

NIGHT ATTACK:
drug traffickers

*dense
jungle*

LAOS

Packbeng

THAILAND

Mekong River

I LEAVE THE CHINESE BEHIND ME.

I take off from the China-Laos border and head towards Luang Namtha. All around me, everything is made of bamboo: the huts, the furniture, the tools, the clotheslines, the chairs, etc. The people have gentle, smiling faces, and direct small, friendly gestures my way, which is almost shocking after China. These women, these children are reawakening my heart. I can see that the jungle is dense; there's no way I'll be able to walk through it! I notice that everyone wears a machete on their backs, stuck under a wide belt, and that they're all wearing flip-flops. I walk into the first shop I see to buy rice. A woman serves me cooked rice, drawn from a marvelous little basket. With her hands, she shapes it into a ball that she puts in a banana leaf. I smile and thank her. Of course, I eat my rice sitting on the side of the country road. But what a brilliant idea, cooked rice! I'm fascinated by all the details, the refined nature of their creations, and by their ingenuity.

At Luang Namtha, I go to a guesthouse. I have to think. I don't want to walk on the roads, I want to go into the jungle. At the moment, this doesn't look promising. I hang out in the road, asking questions, until someone directs me to a young man who speaks perfect English. I explain my problem, and in talking with him, get the idea to go down the river in a canoe. I have to use all my powers of persuasion before he allows me to rent a canoe on my own. I finally succeed at sweet-talking him into a "banana canoe," and soon after find myself floating down the Namtha River. I'm thrilled; it's a tandem canoe, which requires a bit more effort. My backpack occupies the bow, while I navigate through the brown, opaque water. Giant, blue butterflies pass right under my nose, the jungle falls steeply, a wall of green on both banks. I drink in the moment, I'm so happy to be here. I move forward. This requires real upper body work, as there's no current. It's like having front row seats for a show that never ends.

The first night, I find a little spot on the water's edge where I can put up my tent. The second night, two men slip into my camp, pretending to be the police (they had no way of knowing that I'd survived China). Two-person canoe, two-person tent . . . there obviously had to be two occupants. I play the card of the invisible husband: I open my tent a little and pretend to be surprised. I turn and talk to my husband, who's sleeping, and responds in the muffled tones of someone who's just been woken up. This scene lasts a good while, and I see it through. They retreat up the barely visible path that allowed them to find me. At dawn, everything is taken hostage by the jungle fog, even my tent. I know that it will lift all at once, but I don't yet know when, so I wait, observe, listen. I need to learn to read this new scenery.

The next day, small rapids add a little adrenaline to my day. My yellow banana and I relish it. I notice a bit of cleared earth on the bank and decide to settle in for the night and put up my tent. Then I stretch, my shoulders are sore. I carefully empty the canoe without puncturing it. Once my camp is ready, I crawl into my tent, exhausted. All of my muscles ache.

Two hours later, the muscle ache has intensified. Just before my fever surpasses 104°F, I call Gregory in Switzerland with my satellite phone to tell him that I'm coming down with malaria, or dengue fever, or who knows what. I ask him to call my doctor, but no luck—it's Sunday and the doc doesn't pick up. Other options also lead to dead ends. I've brought medicine that I can take, but I want a telephone diagnosis first; these prescriptions are strong. I decide that my only option is to depend on myself, so I prepare a dry wood fire that I don't light, but protect from the damp. I tie my left leg to a tree, knowing that delirium often accompanies high fevers. It's possible that with my head boiling, I'll look for water to cool myself off, and since I'm just a yard from the water's edge, I could fall in. My plan is to make a video every hour, in an effort to stay in touch with reality.

My body very quickly passes into a second phase and icy chills course through my bones. I record myself as my whole body trembles. Little by little, my fever rises to the point where I can no longer touch my eyes or even open them. They feel like they're going to be ejected from their sockets. The fever empties my body of water, so I force myself to drink. I will reach the point where I can no longer speak, but I record a few seconds, dripping with sweat. I know that this will pass, if I can just get through it.

Three days later, I finally open my tent. I can now move slowly without detonating an internal explosion with each step. My entire head is swollen, it feels as though someone has beaten me with a baseball bat . . . but aside from that, I'm better. I call Gregory and ask him to contact the person who rented me the canoe, who promised that he would come get me later if there was a problem. Even so, they take two days to find me!

I recuperate a bit. I decide to set a new course from a village I spotted just before I became ill.

Never sleep near a water source!

Ban Nale is a small village indistinguishable from the others I've seen so far. I climb carefully up through the village and step onto the dirt road that leads out of it. According to my topographic maps, this path crosses the entire jungle and comes out on the eastern side. My body is weak and I advance slowly. The jungle's humidity doesn't help. A bright green snake undulates overhead and I observe his movements and agility as he whips through the palm trees. The trail descends brutally to meet up with a small stream flowing placidly at the bottom of a deep green crevasse, then climbs back up the other side. I religiously follow this path of slippery mud. The fog clings to the summits of the ridges. I navigate by eye, using the indigenous trails.

After a week, I'm spent. The humidity sucks my energy. In

my exhaustion, I break my ironclad rule and set up my tent at the edge of a small pond fed by a hidden stream. I sleep, knocked out cold. Near midnight, I hear voices. I jump and strain to hear; the voices are violent. Suddenly, someone shakes my tent like a plum tree, as if to say, "Hey! Anyone in there?"

I quickly turn on my headlamp and open my tent. I find myself nose-to-nose with several men. The first thing I see are their feet, arrayed in the inevitable flip-flops. Their legs are muscular and dry. These people are very thin, and their coffee-colored skin is dripping sweat. I attempt to greet them kindly while they yell and blind me with bright lights. With my right hand, I push aside the lamp of the man who has decided to conduct the interrogation. What I see sends a chill up my spine. This fellow, the size of a twelve-year-old kid, has a machine gun slung over his shoulder.

I think there must be ten of them, maybe more. It's pitch-black. I don't understand what's happening, but I decide to stand up inside my tent. I figure that since they're small, it might work, so I get up and start yelling at them. The result is swift: they become violent. I sit back down. One guy lifts up my tent with me in it. I hear the tent stakes that fasten the rain fly to the ground shoot off in splinters. They motion for me to go with them.

I rally my mind to action, telling myself, "I absolutely must change this situation, and now!" I plunge my hand into my bag and take out a tiny dictionary that contains the dialects spoken by the various mountain tribes in the region. I open it as the guy with the machine gun gets fed up and discharges a round into the air. His bloodshot eyes seem to want to pop out of his head. In a flash, I understand the gravity of the situation. They're almost certainly drug traffickers who are moving merchandise. The men who had remained calm until now come together and seize everything in front of my tent: camping stove, teapot, hiking poles, cooking pot . . .

I take advantage of the commotion to discreetly get out my tracker. It has an emergency button. Whatever happens, at least my loved ones will know where things ended. Then I read aloud a phrase from the dictionary: "I am a tourist, I am from Switzerland, do you understand me?" I repeat this phrase tirelessly, like a mantra, without stopping, slowly, overarticulating and always with the same intonation. For hours. When I really begin to have enough of this, I sneak a glance at my watch: three o'clock in the morning. Through the dark, I can hear that the men who were to my right are moving and beginning to go back up the little path, leaving only three delegates before me. Is this a good thing? Suddenly, the one who is crouched to my left looks me straight in the eye and says, "We're sorry for the disturbance, ma'am!" These words are pronounced in perfect English. I'm left openmouthed as they disappear into the night, lamps extinguished.

I catch my breath. Well, I'm alive. Whoa! This time, Sarah, things nearly ended in catastrophe!

At first light, I push into the jungle. To my great surprise, I find all of my gear on the path, one piece after another. My teapot here, a hiking pole there, the pot lid a little farther on. In less than half a mile, I find all of it. I giggle to myself, but it rings a bit hollow. I'm still truly shaken. I hurry to get as far away as possible from this place. I haven't slept enough, but the adrenaline is still in my veins, and I make use of it. I don't know where I am, so I navigate by connecting the tiny paths while holding a course to the east.

The women with the silver pipes

As the days pass, I meet the people of the mists, these mountain tribes that live on the summits of the ridges. They come straight from another time. I have unforgettable encounters, like the women who invite me to wash in the stream hidden at the bottom of the valley. I meet a tribe whose entire village greets me by laughing at my face, their only required clothing, a loincloth. As I pass, old women come out from behind bushes, smoking their long, silver pipes, pieces of cloth wound around their heads. Some venture into the jungle to bring back fruits, vegetables, and wild herbs in the nets held fast by a strap across their foreheads and carried on their backs. Others, where the altitude allows it, practice slash-and-burn agriculture.

Click or no click?

When I come in contact with these people who have the privilege of living secluded from the world, I choose not to take pictures. The moment lived has often been so vibrant and authentic that I've decided to keep only the mental image. I've seen giraffe-women penned up in fake villages where the tourists paid to take pictures. I've seen globe-trotting tourists steal photos of a grandmother who was bathing naked in a mountain village in Thailand. The list is long. These intrusions are sad and easily avoided, to say nothing of the total lack of respect and infringement on the person's liberties. I've noticed that I don't fully live the present moment while I'm nagging myself to figure out when I'm going to take a photo, and from what angle, what light. I miss the magic of the moment.

I leave these mountains after weeks of slogging. I'm ready for a shower and a stir-fry of rice and vegetables! It's early afternoon, I arrive in a village at the edge of the paved main road that will take me to the Thai border. Impatient to get there, I pick up the pace when suddenly, at the entrance to the village, a man on a motorcycle in the shade of a building calls out, "Oh, where are you from?" I turn around without stopping and respond, in French, "I don't understand, sorry," and keep moving straight ahead. I smile because while turning back around, I see a gigantic red sign stating, "Access forbidden to foreigners."

I mix with the people in the market square for safety and come out on the other side, where I find a little room at the far end of the village. I take a shower and eat fried rice with vegetables and lime zest, sitting on the ground in front of the stoop of my little room. I begin to feel like myself again. The hens scratch the dirt in the courtyard. I'm safe for the night.

I progress along this road. Then one day, at the day's end, I find myself before the legendary Mekong River. I'm in southern Laos, the sun stretches to the west while small, elongated boats with loud motors carry their passengers across the river. On the opposite bank lies Thailand.

10. Thailand

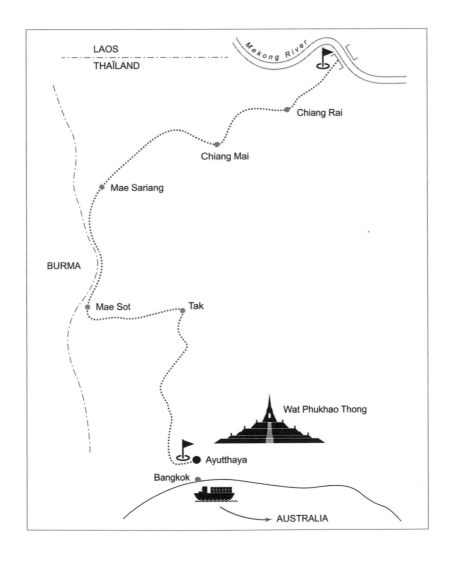

UNTIL NOW, I HAVE AVOIDED THE SOURCE OF ALL MY problems, people; but Thailand will tame me with its smiles, its monks, its scents, and its generosity. The paths that span the country guide me westward, as I'd hoped. I thread my way through these mountains that are much less difficult than the Laotian jungle, even with their drops and climbs that sometimes defy the laws of gravity. From the first weeks, I'm fascinated by the friendliness of the locals. It's surprising. I'm invited to share meals with all sorts of people, they give me water without my asking for it. . . . I feel like I'm part of their community.

I find the placement of the temples situated in the mountains impressive. Gigantic golden buddhas materialize in the jungle in the most unexpected places. I meet monks in the forest, meditating under a tree. Thailand is so different from every part of my trip until now! It's rare to walk more than a day without finding food—which, after all the battles I had to fight just to feed myself, seems strange. I spend days walking alongside rice paddies. And yet I feel tired, exhausted. I have to fight just to do nine-mile days before getting to my resupply point.

I arrive in Chiang Mai, where my expedition chief is waiting for me. I'm a bundle of nerves, the traffic and pollution of the city hit me like a ton of bricks. Gregory gives me my supplies, takes care of my ongoing business, and leaves. I'm going to stay a little longer, I need to recuperate. Just to be sure, I decide to go to the clinic for foreigners to have a blood test done. The results are quick and the doctor, very professional, delivers them with humor. "It's not at all serious, you just need an extra-strength deworming. Just like what we'd give to dogs." I laugh at her good humor. But, indeed, my insides are overrun with worms. She puts me on an IV drip to rehydrate my body. In her hands she holds a syringe filled with red liquid, another that's transparent, a yellow one, and two others whose colors I don't remember. She injects me with the totality of these emergency vitamin infusions. I feel like I'm coming out of the garage, where the tune-up was thoroughly and exquisitely done. I thank her and get back on the road.

Rice on all sides

I realize that my steps have followed the complete cycle of rice: planting in China, harvest in Laos, then ploughing and planting young shoots in Thailand. The irrigation canals connecting the rice paddies allow the water to fill them at a slow pace. The water runs everywhere with enthusiasm, as though it's been held back, like old water finding its young legs. But it had to wait while the buffalos trampled and turned over the muddy earth with all their might, pulling a plough, basic in design but effective in this type of soil. After a few days, water covers everything. Suddenly, an aquatic life springs up. The surface of the water ripples, amphibians try to escape from hunters posted there by chance. The sunset is reflected in this giant mirror formed by the meticulously leveled terraces formed at different heights to let the water naturally overflow from one to the other.

A silhouette appears in the distance, moving so slowly that it seems to float above the glare. The water buffalo smell me well before the dogs or the humans do. Silently, their nostrils dilate, sniffing me from a good distance. I see their heads, coiffed with their half-moon horns, look for me in the landscape. Their movements are so slow that they make me think of gigantic guardians of time. So I put down my pack nearby and spend some time humming them a melody that's well-traveled, telling of other lands, other smells. These scenes remind me of the coming and going of the cows of my village, who had the same schedule as the commuters, still half asleep behind the wheels of their cars. The drivers would curse these slow and gentle creatures that the farmer's stick never made move any faster. My mother always found this reassuring, and each time we were blocked on the road by the various herds that crossed our small village of five hundred people, she would observe them with wonder, as though they were exotic animals. During this time, through her, I learned little by little to see past appearances.

The intense orange of the long, carefully coiled cloths dress the bodies of the monks. They're present, just there, in the scenery. I get used to it on the surface but, inside me, these fluttering robes and closely shaved heads leave a mark without explanation. Our eyes meet often. We each try to decipher the other, so different are we by our accoutrements. But one day, when the temperature is dangerously high, I run into a wandering monk with his parasol and his offering bowl slung over his shoulder. His bare feet have become just a thick crust of skin. He greets me, bringing his hands together in front of his chest, and I do the same. From the sleeves of his robe he draws a cold tea as well as a bottle of water. With one finger, he points at the sun. I understand and accept the beverages. After noon, a monk may neither eat nor drink. The sun is at its zenith, so he can't drink according to their rule and prefers to give me his beverages.

I later learn that wandering monks and all those who've chosen to follow a simple life of poverty are admired and cherished. To have someone like this in your home is an honor and good karma for the family. I don't wear orange robes, but in the eyes of the Thai people, my effort and my approach have never seemed strange. No one here ever asks me the inevitable question, "Why do you walk?"

I'm now bursting with energy and I devour mile after mile, despite the temperature. I'm nearing the Burmese border. Suddenly a car stops and a familiar face appears. "How am I supposed to bring you chocolate in this heat?" I burst out laughing, it's Loyse Pahud who has come to join me for four days of walking. She's a journalist for the magazine *Femina* who's covered my entire expedition. I have a wonderful time with her; we laugh a lot, and our adventures, though short, are not insignificant. An elephant invites itself into our camp one evening on the banks of a river, we make campfires, jump into streams after long, strenuous days and, during all of this, she always has a smile on her face. Once, she even thought she saw a bear in our camp, but it turned out to be just a piece of wood. . . .

I have with me someone who's completely open to her environment and it's here that the key to all adaptation lies. At night, in her tent, she's fascinated by the sounds of the jungle, the rustling. Our laughter must still be caught in the trees of each of the camps we made. *Thank you, thank you . . .*

The temperature rises above 105°F with ninety percent humidity. The horizon is never clear; it's the season when people burn the ground to stimulate regrowth or to take over a corner of the forest, a piece of earth. I avoid these wildfires and head into the mountains that are now inhabited by a mix of people from different cultures. Clothing changes colors, women style their thick, black hair according to their tradition, and add silver ornamentation.

The border is well-defined: on one side Thailand, on the other Burma. But in looking at these people's appearances, you understand that these mountains form a whole. On Route 105, which stretches along the dangerous frontier, I run into pirates who steal only the large pineapple I've attached to my cart, right in front. I come down from the mountains via Tak. The heat is stifling and is here to stay. The population becomes more dense, I'm nearing my goal. I take refuge inside temple walls; I'll be safe there to spend the night in my tent.

Ayutthaya—Wat Phukhao Thong, May 6, 2012

I cross the region devastated by the floods of 2011. Water is still abnormally present here and there. Nature has adapted to a more aquatic environment in the months that have followed, which explains the presence of monstrous lizards that furtively cross the road between scooters. These scenes are entertaining and endlessly surprising! And then there's the lotus that's proliferated. Its extreme elegance touches me and gives me the necessary energy to get to Ayutthaya.

Here, it's the end of the day like any other. A woman approaches with tired steps, pushing a cart. I spot my destination, the temple Phukhao Thong. Firmly rooted in the terrain, yet shooting high into the air, it dominates its surroundings. It's flanked by rice paddies in which the clouds like to gaze upon their own reflected sparkle. I keep walking as my tears begin to fall. I stop at the steps which seem to rise to the sky. I'm here, I've arrived, and I'm alive! I just crossed Asia on foot.

My emotions cannot be contained, I continue to cry. I place

there, at the foot of this temple, an abstract of my efforts in the form of tears.

Cargo ship, single woman on board

I've boarded a merchant cargo ship with twenty-two German and Filipino crew members; I'm the only woman on board. Throughout the thirteen days at sea, I impatiently fix on the horizon to the south. We pass the equator, its air saturated with moisture, and I remember feeling a chill seeing the onboard GPS show 000:000:000, indicating that we were traveling over the waistline of Earth. Thirteen days later, the port of Brisbane is in view. I'm happy to arrive in Australia by sea, it's a nod to all the people who once left everything behind and arrived by boat.

Australia has always been my destination!

11. Northern Australia

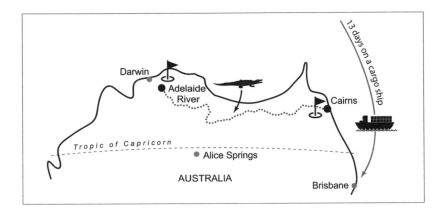

Tears the aroma of coffee . . .

IT'S MAY 28, 2012, AND I HURRY TO PULL MY TWO HUGE trekking bags out of my cabin and make my way to the lower deck. My bags are heavy, they carry my precious cart, dismantled for the voyage, and all the rest of my gear. I go wait in front of the gangplank, barely able to contain my excitement. With a big smile, a Filipino sailor tosses one of my bags on his back while I take care of the other. He climbs down the narrow, detachable ladder, and I follow on his heels. Forty-three steps later, my feet touch the soil of the port of Brisbane, Australia.

For security reasons, they drive me to the entrance of the docks in a minibus. Then a taxi brings me into town. I leave my belongings in a small boardinghouse at 405 Upper Edward Street. I chat with the owner who has a hard time understanding why I spent thirteen days at sea on a cargo ship. "Oh, you

Australians!" I exclaim, looking at him. He remains stoic, so I decide to avoid giving him a heart attack and don't tell him where I've gone the past two years, let alone what I was doing! I don't have time to hang around, though, I have an appointment that I wouldn't miss for anything. I walk with a light step downtown, passing the familiar bronze statues in front of city hall, and come out in the pedestrian area. I spot a coffee shop and sit down at an outdoor table. I order a café latte. The waiter has a large, welcoming smile, and asks me how I'm doing this morning. I smile back and reply, "Incredibly well!" He puts in my order. I gaze happily at the coffee that he brings me. It's perfect, full of foam, just as I'd imagined it so many times. I take the cup in my hands as though it were a precious and fragile object and take a sip. I close my eyes and smile. The pleasure this moment brings me is beyond words; I've waited two years to have a café latte.

The places I've been in the last two years didn't offer this kind of delicacy. This appointment with my first cup of coffee makes me realize how full of pitfalls, pain, and sweat the path that's led me here has been. I end up sitting for five hours, drinking coffee and people watching. I become aware that, for once, I melt into the crowd. All around me, there are lots of "Long Noses" with white skin, and no Asians. No one gives me judgmental or questioning looks. I breathe deeply; I'm among my own people. For the first time in twenty years, I intimately understand my belonging to the ethnic group known as Caucasian.

I go to my Australian bank to reactivate my account. A young bank teller serves me and gets right to work on my account. He remarks that I've been a loyal client for over twenty years. He asks me what brings me once again to Queensland. I explain that I'm going to walk from Cairns to Darwin. He looks at me, terrified, and responds, "You're crazy!" He's very young and terribly serious, he's not joking around . . . and neither am I.

I've been in Cairns for a few days and I've been able to get all I need for my departure, including new water containers. I've also asked around for a good osteopath, and have benefited from massages that, after so much time walking, do my body endless good. I've left all my gear in a cheap room above a car rental agency. Rosy, the boss, helped with my preparations and has agreed to keep one of my big bags. I tell her that my expedition leader will pick it up in a few months. On the eve of my departure, she finds me a seat on a friend's minibus that's headed north with tourists. The driver has agreed to drop me off at my point of departure, thirty minutes north of town, which will save me the price of a taxi. The next morning, as planned, I'm waiting at the bus stop on Spencer Street. It's 6:30 a.m., a minibus stops, and George gets out and welcomes me enthusiastically. The good humor and smiles of the people here do me good; I'd forgotten how welcoming Australians are. A half hour later, George leaves me exactly where I asked, by the seashore, in the middle of nowhere. "Where are you going from here?" he asks.

I get out my map and show him the route I've chosen to follow, which goes deep into the bush and rises steeply to the top of a plateau fifty miles away. He gives me a big hug and wishes me good luck. He takes a few steps toward his bus, then turns back and adds, "Don't worry, the bush will protect you. This is the land of my people, the Yirrganydji." He tells me that the totem of this terrain is the dingo. I watch him drive off, then enter the bush, which, from my first steps, surrounds me with its familiar scents and sounds. I feel like I've come home. The emotion is overwhelming after two years in hostile lands, and silent tears flow down my cheeks. *Thank you, thank you . . .*

That evening, after a hard day of pulling my cart on a steep and craggy path, I fall asleep without eating, exhausted both physically and emotionally. This first night I dream of my dog D'Joe, whom I miss greatly. He has the big, red-brown body of a raptor, and he shows me that feathers have grown on the underside of his wings. I can sense that he's ready to take flight. This is the last time that I'll dream of him.

My days and nights come directly out of a fairy tale. To start with, I don't see a soul, since access to this path is prohibited. A big iron bar across the road blocks all motorized vehicles. To my great pleasure, I share this wilderness with all sorts of birds, kangaroos, and lots of small mammals and snakes. That night, I arrive at the plateau at the top of the Tablelands. A small area of the bush has intentionally been burned, and at the foot of this zone winds a pretty little creek. I decide to put up my tent and stock up on water. All around my camp, there are dense plants much taller than I am and tall trees arrayed in various types of vegetation. Night falls very quickly and by five o'clock, it's dark. I'm lying in my tent, listening to the lively nighttime activity, with noises that come from the ground, but also sounds emitted by the trees, which inspire the imagination. I've always dreamed of having night vision. . . . Suddenly a hoarse, hollow sound rings out with such force that it makes me jump. All the other sounds stop. I don't know its author, and yet it's right there, behind my tent. Its steps are quiet but audible, and spaced apart. The heavy, authoritative call glides easily out into the night. I use the process of elimination to determine its origin. The wild pig, which is apparently common in this region, comes to mind, but I know its call, and this isn't it. I go through all the possible inhabitants of this environment. In the silence of my tent, at the heart of this dark night, the name of the intruder comes to me. I've never encountered one before. It goes down to the creek a few yards from my tent. I follow it with my ears. I'm truly fortunate to stumble upon it like this, it's the king of the rainforest: the highly respected cassowary or *Casuarius casuarius*. It's a sort of big emu whose neck is brilliantly colored red and turquoise, an astonishing animal that feeds mostly on fruits and doesn't hesitate to kill its enemies with its powerful claws. I track it, listening closely, for a good part of the night. A few days after this event, it's June 20, I'm forty years old, and it's been two years since I began my expedition. It's a day like any other, with sweat, miles, and aches on the agenda. And yet, I'm happy.

I cross the fog-bathed Misty Mountains, where green dominates. I'm on the lookout for the smallest sounds. Here lives the very rare arboreal kangaroo, *Dendrolagus lumholtzi*. Each night I sleep on the floor of this heavy, damp forest, surrounded by creatures that brush against my tent during the night. At this day's end, I'm wet to the bone: the sun couldn't be bothered to come dry me out during the day, as it's done so regularly until now. This forest doesn't look like the ones before it, even in the daylight it's dark and dense. The climbs have been substantial since this morning, to the point where, as soon as I stop, I'm cold. So I avoid taking breaks. But now I'm hungry, thirsty, and my bones are aching because of the humidity. I desperately look for a ten-foot-square patch of ground to plant my tent. I decide to test my luck and settle for a tiny spur of land. My tent won't be ideally attached, but it will hold. Water now falls from the sky insistently. I can't even open my umbrella, the branches make it impossible. I put up my tent as quickly as possible. Suddenly an enormous, fat snake glides down from a tree right there in front of me, and then continues on its merry way. It's almost dark and, soaked to the bone, I take refuge in my tent. Once inside, I turn on my headlamp to find that I'm not alone, but accompanied by yellow and black leeches. I make myself some good, hot tea and dump in one of the trusty packets of noodles I've brought for just this kind of occasion. Almost instantly, I forget the selfish kisses of the tigresses attached to my flesh. I'll go over the tent inch-by-inch before sleeping to be sure that they don't spend the night dining at my expense.

I arrive in the small town of Ravenshoe with a clear mission. During my 2002–2003 expedition in Australia, I met an old gold prospector named George who lived in the bush and taught me a lot. If I remember right, one of his friends came from Ravenshoe and resupplied him once a week. I'd like to hear how he's doing, so I stop at the first pub I see to ask about him. The young women behind the counter aren't Australian, so they won't be any help. I go into a second pub, this one more old-fashioned. The bartender can't help me with my search, but she gapes at me and exclaims, "It seems that you could really use one of our showers first, honey!" I jump at her offer, thanking her more than I need to. When I reappear, she doesn't recognize me. It's not until I return the bath linens she kindly lent me that she realizes that it's me and can't help laughing at the extreme transformation. In the meantime, she conducted her little investigation among the regulars and directs me toward two old blokes drinking their stubbies in a corner. I introduce myself and tell them my story. It turns out that they knew George "the Irishman," but they give me the sad news that he died a few months earlier. I'll never know if it was really him. But I send him a thought, in remembrance of our encounter.

I go to the café at the edge of the village with the distinct image of George in my head. I fill my belly with food—and a café latte, of course—until it can't hold any more. The women at the table opposite me have been staring at me for awhile, so I strike up a conversation. They're the kind of people who know everything about everything for miles around. I decide to play their game and sum up my adventures. They jump in their seats when I tell them about the yellow and black leeches. "What, you're sleeping in the scrub?" Suddenly, an uncomfortable silence descends, then one of the four bravely speaks up in a hushed voice, looking over her shoulder to be sure that no one's listening. "You know there are all kinds of bizarre things in the forest. . . ." And she tells me why, when they were kids, no one dared to go there. The story would stay between them and me—I promised I wouldn't tell a soul! The chubbier of the women ends the exchange saying, "You're lucky you ran into us, kid."

Then their discussion continues as though our little conversation had never taken place.

In a voice now calm, the woman declares, "Do you know what? This morning, one of my hens was strolling down my front walkway when . . ."

The rest of the conversation mixes with the sounds of chairs being moved around, new patrons coming and going, and then it's time for me to go.

That night, I find a pretty, well-hidden campsite far from the village at the edge of a magnificent stream. In the early morning hours of the following day, squatting at the edge of the stream and contemplating the beauty that surrounds me, I brush my teeth. Suddenly a man comes out of the tall grass three yards away. I quickly stand up, instinctively, like a wild animal. My toothbrush hasn't left my mouth. I chew it nervously without realizing it. A pair of laughing blue eyes look at me with a charming smile. "Would you join me for a cup of tea? I'm just down there below the stream." I stare at him like an eight-year-old girl. I remain mute. In front of me is a man who looks dangerously like Robert Redford in his younger days. It takes me a few seconds to come back to my senses. I'm not facing down a threatening Mongolian or a drug trafficker. I'm simply confronted by the woman inside me, she's suddenly surfaced like a lioness with all the emotions that go along with it. Perhaps I'm so blindsided by this because the men I met in Asia didn't catch my eye. The man is still watching me, not a sound has come out of my mouth, which is still very busy chewing on my toothbrush. After some seconds, which must have seemed to him like minutes, I pull myself together and quickly remove the toothbrush. Now I just have to discreetly get rid of the contents of my mouth. I smile and blush at the same time, picking up where he left off. "You really shouldn't barge into my bathroom without knocking!" He laughs and replies, "I think I just realized that!"

I thank him for the invitation, but refuse. We spend a good

hour chatting, with me being secretly disconcerted by those too-blue eyes, until I reach my limit. I stand up and signal the end of our conversation. I ditch him there and dive into the tall grass to take refuge in my camp, well camouflaged and sheltered from curious eyes.

My days become a gentle repetition of nearly total tranquility. Solitude alone is there to soothe me. The dread of being stalked by sinister characters long ago departed my days and nights . . . which doesn't mean that I want to run into people. I always hide for my own safety. Sometimes I wake up in the middle of the bush with great bulls by my side, lying down like lambs, or even kangaroos, which are becoming less and less fearful. My energy is calm and serene. Is this why birds come right up to me? I've reached the region where little towers rise out of the ground. It's the work of termites. They fascinate me, they can survive almost anything. Inside their nest, underground, peat is maintained at the right temperature and the ideal humidity to make fungus grow. This reserve will feed the entire colony. I spend hours observing the dozens of species of ants, from the fat black ones with the shiny backsides, to the elegant purple ones. Often I fall asleep under a tree when the temperature becomes unbearable, letting them run across my body with delight.

The transformation slips in, settles, nibbles away just there, under my skin, with each step. Insignificant and faceless at first. Then, slowly, my molecules react, begin to tickle me. My path is there, drawn beneath my skin, it's the reflection of the exterior. Each step taken is conscious. During this time, the intellect lives its life. Until the day that the trees nourish me, and everything is part of a whole. Two years have put me in a blur . . . and now the fog suddenly lifts, the edges become clear, the colors seem perfect. My transformation took all these steps, all this time. Today I realize that nature lives within me, I am she, she is part of me. Whoa . . . I spend days digesting this harmonic energy with Mother Nature that's so difficult to describe. To be face-to-face with her sensitivity often means finding oneself completely naked. The incomprehension of those and of that which surrounds us builds in us like a frustration, an army of little soldiers who, one day, rebel without declaring war. The most beautiful gift you can give someone is to listen. This allows them to manage the little soldiers inside them. Because they're just there to protect you. Once you get past that stage, another world opens up.

As for me, I'm surrounded by trees with familiar silhouettes, succeeded by flat sections of plains with tall grasses blanched by the scorching sun. It's very early in the morning, a Brahma bull jumps the fence like a gazelle. He looks at me and continues on his way with a casual step. I'm fascinated by these massive, ungainly creatures that somehow manage to embody such elegance. I learned to love these ingenious beasts during my 8,700-mile expedition from 2002 to 2003. I shared water sources with them, saw moms take turns calf sitting—one mother watching as many as eight calves at one time. I shared nights and many moments of peace by their side. The only question I wonder about is this: how can one kill such a beautiful creature to eat? I'll continue to ask myself this question without fear of seeming stupid. How many times have I been brushed aside when I've broached the subject. . . . "We can't avoid it," someone inevitably explains, "That's life!" Or even, "What do you think we should eat? Nuts and berries?" These are the easy answers that people throw back at me. The conversation always ends in ugly, mocking laughter. So, to answer this question, I decided to see if I could hunt in order to feed myself. For so many years, it's been drummed into me that I'm a carnivore and that I have teeth made for eating meat, etc. And so I hunted to feed myself, to survive. I knew true hunger, I killed my prey with my own hands, I fully lived my place in the food chain.

So yes, I've experienced it, and I've personally chosen to have the least impact possible on this earth, to cause the least amount of suffering possible. This is my choice. We're all free . . . for a little while longer, at least. The problem is that our society lives in an imaginary bubble. We eat horse meat and exclaim, "It's so tender!" But are we capable of touching a horse, of looking it in the eye before positioning it for slaughter, then feeling the life leave its body? Of plunging our hands in its still-warm blood, so we can carve from its flesh this small bit of meat that's so tender? Through hunting, I discovered that in order to feed yourself and earn your food, you really have to be brave. Because inflicting death isn't an innocent act. We're in complete denial of our own functioning within our habitat—to the point where, for years, upon announcing that I was a vegetarian, people would respond, "So you eat chicken?" I realized that these people had never seen or touched a chicken. I've been a vegetarian since I was eleven years old. It happened at dinner with my family while I was eating sausage. Following a comment on the origin of this sausage, reality struck like a lightning bolt: I understood that there on my plate was my childhood friend, "Moumou." This ewe had grown up with me and I had visited her every day in the pasture. One cold night, in a make-shift shelter, I'd watched my father help her lamb her two little ones. Yes, I was eating a member of my family.

Since that day, I've understood that every life should be protected and cherished. We lose empathy toward our own race, toward the animal kingdom. The human is sick, overweight, we overconsume, we kill more, we pollute more. We pollute Earth, and therefore the air we breathe, and the climate heats up. But we don't want to see it, so what to do?

I've chosen my camp: I'm a vegetarian. But this wasn't enough for me. I needed to experience it myself to understand. I've walked the equivalent of the perimeter of Earth without eating meat—with one exception: during my previous expedition in Australia when I wanted to know if I was capable of providing food for myself by my own hand. I surpassed my physical limits, I was exposed to the harshest elements of the earth and to hunger, with nothing but nuts and berries in my pack for nourishment. And so, after more than thirty years without meat, while leading the physically demanding life of an explorer, I'm living proof that it's possible to live without killing another being!

I want to share with you this incredible story.

It takes place in New South Wales, Australia. It's the beginning of summer, 2002. I'm walking on the Great Dividing Range, which is a chain of mountains set back from the coast. The bush is incredibly dense with old eucalyptus which, like motionless statues, emerge from the rest of the vegetation that crawls at their feet. The spot has the kind of beauty that takes away your breath, the air is already dry for the season, and the aromas given off by the trees dominate the breeze. A man is engaged in hand-to-hand combat with a section of livestock fencing. I come closer and call out, "Who's winning?" Surprised, he turns around and drops the wire strainer he holds in his hands. "This is the third time this month I've had to fix this fence, damn it! It's time for a bite to eat, are you coming to the house?"

This human warmth that the people who live in the bush exude has always surprised me and always will surprise me. I accept his invitation and accompany him to the farm, where we find his wife and four children. He invites me to follow him inside. He officially marks his break, hanging his cowboy hat by the door. I sit down at the family table with everyone else and we devour what in my country we call "a four o'clock," otherwise known as a snack. His wife is wonderful and genuine, their smiles are generous and true. We have a lively conversation. Suddenly, I look at the husband and ask him the question that's been burning on my lips since I saw him: "Where are your cows?" His wife bursts out laughing, and begins to tell me the story of her husband.

He came home one day, shocked and shaken, after loading up the last truck of livestock destined for the slaughterhouse. He looked his wife straight in the eye and told her, "I can't do it anymore. I can't watch them go to slaughter, I love them too much." Since that day, with the support of his wife, he's stopped raising livestock. The whole family decided to build a series of cabins to host people who wanted to experience nature firsthand. "Now, the client can wake up in the morning in the bush with the birds, and all the magic that goes with it," the husband proudly tells me with a broad smile. I congratulate them, I'm so happy to meet such brave folks. The father ends the story like this: "I'd arrived at the point of no return! There was no possible compromise. So we started a new life!"

This family has greatly inspired me in my life. And shown by example that a total change is possible at any moment. *Thank you, thank you . . .*

Queensland, July 16, 2012

I leave my belongings under an old bridge. I'm safely hidden there. I unlace my shoes out of habit, then put them down carelessly. A few minutes later, I hear the water in my teapot quivering, and I stretch out on the mattress of sand that this old dry creek bed offers me and blissfully plunge my bare feet into it. I close my eyes for a moment and . . . I hear a murmur: *I would have liked for you to soak your tired legs in the water that once was. . . . But everyone used it up, you see: the kangaroos, the lizards, the livestock, and also the clouds and the stars who liked to reflect themselves in it. You can still see the tracks in the sand, some of them still visit me, they remember the beauty of my water.* The murmur continues: *You know, one day, my edges appeared, then everything accelerated. Today, I offer you what's left of me, but know that each grain of sand possesses the memory of my emerald colored water.* The sound of the water overflowing in my teapot pulls me from my mini slumber. I make my tea and look at my feet buried in this creek bed. I feel the coolness rise up through my legs (the grains of sand are telling me their story). I smile silently as I swallow my first sip of tea. The topographic map gives my location: I'm in the bed of Crystal Creek.

That morning, I come out of the bush after an amazing night amid bloodwood trees and surrounded by ocher-red termites and tall white grasses. The birds went on with their lives without paying much attention to my presence, which brought me beautiful moments, lying in the grasses, observing their acrobatic flights. It's these moments that I cherish more than anything.

I start my day with not one, but three crossings of barbed-wire fences. This means serious effort of carrying, sliding, rolling, etc. I put my pack back on and continue on my way. Fallen trees and dense vegetation in some spots force me to carry all my gear. This morning is more like an obstacle course designed to train marines than the activity known as "walking." And then I find myself at a road. As I'm crossing, my cart makes a strange sound of metal clanging together. I stop and discover that all the spokes on one of my wheels are completely loose, and others aren't attached at all. I can't be mad at my poor cart, this morning's terrain was incredibly rough. I put everything down in the glaring sun, and I think. Suddenly, a pickup truck appears on the horizon. I wave my arms, signaling for him to stop. Apparently, they're wild pig killers. If I had to classify the danger of people you meet in the bush, I'd put them at the top of the list. Damn! Truly unlucky. In the back are two exhausted dogs, muzzles bloody, and the blood hasn't yet had time to dry. . . . I know this type. I directly get their attention by asking for a monkey wrench to repair my wheel. They lend me one and, after a long moment watching me painstakingly tighten my spokes, the driver decides to keep going, leaving me the precious tool. "Well, at least they were nice," I think, watching them drive off. It takes me over an hour to tighten all the spokes, the monkey wrench being way too big for them. Gently, patiently, I finally finish and temporarily fix the problem. I'm twenty miles from Normanton, I hope that it will hold.

I arrive the following day at this village that I already know from having stopped here during my last expedition ten years ago. I immediately call Switzerland to order a new set of wheels. Barely an hour later, everything is set up for my wheels to be delivered. At best, it will take seven days for them to get to Cairns and God knows how many days more before I receive them here, over four hundred miles from Cairns. I take the hit. But I don't want to be stuck here, I'll go nuts. I run up to the first person I see, who confirms that a bus serves Normanton twice a week. I leave my tent in the back of a motel and hurry to find the bus schedule. I'm absurdly lucky, it's leaving very early the next morning. I get the lady at the motel to agree to keep my belongings, and at dawn, I get on the bus. After more than seven hours, I arrive in Cairns, my gaiters still on my feet, not having washed in weeks. I get off the bus and walk to Rosy's place, to see if she can rent me the same little room. I feel like I'm coming down from another planet.

One week later, I return as planned to Normanton with my new wheels under my arm. I'm truly happy to be back, I feel grimy from the bustle of the city and I'm impatient to get back to the bush. I leave the next day, escorted over the first mile by Jonas, a young Swiss guy on bicycle whom I found completely lost the evening before. The irony of our meeting is that he'd contacted me by e-mail to get information about Australia before leaving, and here we've run into each other in the middle of nowhere! We laugh about it, he speaks hardly any English, and he reminds me of myself when I was very young, not knowing a word of English when I landed in Australia for the first time. But he's crossing Australia powered by his calves, so I describe the difficulties he'll encounter as well as the beauty he should be sure not to miss. That morning, he accompanies me on foot until we reach an intersection. He continues eastward while I head into what the locals call "the dust plains."

The grevilleas are still in bloom, and I take full advantage. I take short breaks that consist of finding this flower in the shape of an elegant brush, between three and six inches long and orange-yellow in color. I check to be sure there aren't any insects on it and I suck the nectar that's a transparent syrup gathered at the base of the flower. This is how I enjoy this rare, sweet little bush treat. I'm very careful not to damage the flower before moving on to the next one. The scene might look a bit odd, seen from the outside. But for me, it's an exquisite delicacy.

I make camp in a little basin carved in the top of the bank of a stagnant pond, when suddenly shots whistle past my ears, out of nowhere. . . . I'm being shot at! I throw myself to the ground and don't move until dawn. I leave this depression in the ground which certainly saved my life and get back to the sandy, reddish-brown path. After barely ten minutes, I find a camp of wild pig hunters. I told you these guys were dangerous!

These guys here are still asleep, and I slip into the landscape and melt into the bush. Most of the time, they're drunk. That day, I cover twenty miles to reach my water source, Leichhardt Falls.[6] I arrive drenched in sweat, red as a tomato, and with

---

6. Ludwig Leichhardt (1813–1848) was an explorer and naturalist who braved these crocodile-infested rivers during an expedition from October 1, 1944 to December 17, 1945. He traveled from Jimbour (near Brisbane) to Port Essington (185 miles north of Darwin).

barely ten ounces left in my water bottle. The place has a dramatic flair: the appearance of these red cliffs that unveil themselves only during the dry season makes you feel as though you're violating the privacy of a grand dame. The water is just a trickle. The rainy season is coming, and then it will be a whole different story. Then, it will look like a basin that's overflowing everywhere in the midst of wild animals, birds, and greenery, all of it bathed in the deafening noise of the thirty-foot falls. From Normanton westward, toward the frontier with the Northern Territories, all access can be blocked for three months or more, depending on the year. Torrential rains cover everything during the rainy season, and only those animals and livestock that take refuge on higher ground survive. It's the cycle of nature that regenerates everything in its path. The farmers here open all the gates of the various paddocks so that, a few days before the rains, the cattle migrate instinctively toward the highest places.

I set up my camp as far back as possible and go to cool off where the water flows over a rock before making its thirty-foot descent into the lower basin. I'm on the lookout, the invisible king of this area is none other than the most formidable crocodile: the saltwater crocodile, *Crocodylus porosus*. I see the upper basin's brown water stir on the surface, indicating the invisible presence of an inhabitant. I later learn that this place is also populated with sharks (bull sharks and school sharks) and that, according to the farmers, some of them reach lengths of eleven feet.[7]

I draw my water with caution and am checking out the site without getting too close to the bank, when suddenly a big black

---

7. In the 1970s, the farmer at Floraville Station (farm) remembers having seen an Aborigine kill a six-foot-long bull shark with a spear.

dog comes out of nowhere and rubs against my leg with laughing little eyes. I give him a big hug, which he milks for all it's worth. I take my time and give him a massage—just like my dog D'Joe would ask me to do each evening after a long day of walking. This dog is wearing a collar marked "Floraville." According to my maps, it's the name of the farm upstream of the falls. The dog looks at me with eyes that say, "Wow, I've never felt this before, go on, go on!" He makes me laugh, and the more I laugh, the more he plays it up. He gets up, rubs against me a little more, then contentedly continues on his way.

Early the next morning, I cross the tributary that feeds the falls on a causeway. The causeway is almost even with the water's surface, and it facilitates the crossing of (mostly) vehicles. For me, this ford is easy, I don't have to worry about crocodiles; the water is so low that the causeway is dry. The cowboys in the old days had a technique to avoid losing cattle at crocodile-infested river crossings: they'd send a scout to crack his whip at the surface of the water, which was enough to scare off the predators that regularly culled an animal here and there from the herd. It often happens when an animal is getting ready to drink and leans forward. I arrive at the other side with dry feet.

There are forty-eight miles still to go before Burketown. The plain is deserted, there's not a tree on the horizon, and it's about 86°F. It's winter, which is the dry season. I use my umbrella to protect myself from the sun whenever I stop. The Australian sun is blistering, I protect myself meticulously, applying SPF 50 sunscreen to my face several times a day and wearing a broad-brimmed hat that covers me completely, which I only take off when I go into my tent at night. I wear long sleeves, so no part of my skin is exposed except my hands.

The next day, I come across workmen performing maintenance on the pipeline that crosses this plain. After a few minutes, they take pity on me and offer me their lunch box! Inside, I find an apple and a hamburger, which I eat with delight, except for the ground meat. And so, with exceptional energy, I race off to arrive in Burketown at the end of the day. It's the last little town in the vicinity, the next one is 650 miles west. I'm glad to be here. I go straight to the campground to wash myself and all my gear. On the to-do list: write a blog post on the last section of my journey, call Switzerland, and buy groceries.

This little village of two hundred inhabitants is more or less trapped between two river systems: to the west is the Nicholson River, to the east, the impressive Albert River. The inhabitants are at once isolated from the world and exposed to cyclones, which close them off for months during the rainy season. Airplane and helicopter are the only ways to get out in case of emergency. The two workmen I met informed me, with great sadness in their voices, that the village pub had burned down just a few weeks ago, and that there was no beer to be found in the whole town. I can't help but laugh! Ah, the Australians and their stubbies. I settle in at the campground where they welcome me like a VIP. Australia has changed so much: ten years ago, during one of my previous expeditions, they regarded me with disgust and incredulity. Today no one says, "that's impossible!" each time I tell them about my journey. Instead they ask, "How far are you going?" Australians have opened themselves to the world, for better and for worse.

In the basic but clean campground restroom, I meet Peggy,

the kind of woman I immediately take a liking to, eyes bright and full of lively sparkle, cloaked in a tired and bulky body. She lives with her husband at the campground during the months when they dedicate themselves to fishing for barramundi (in my opinion, the tastiest fish there is). I notice that Peggy doesn't look me in the eye when she talks to me, but focuses on a point just to the left of my face. I find her behind the building in the middle of hanging her laundry out to dry. I'm doing a load of laundry and, while waiting, flip through old *People* magazines that folks have left there, like the vestiges of a distant civilization where movie actresses in evening gowns pose, hand on hip. I burst out laughing. Peggy turns around and asks what's going on. I'm surprised that she was able to hear me from so far away without seeing me. Now it's her turn to burst out laughing, and she comes over with her bag of clothespins. "Sarah, I'm blind!" She sits down and tells me her story. At seventy-eight, she has a lovely self-assuredness, and she's a survivor. I'm inspired by her courage, her life's path. I thank her. Her husband calls her to come for her afternoon cup of tea. It's time to hang out my laundry.

Snake, dust, and cloud . . .

This morning, I leave Burketown with enough food to get me to the next general store, which is in an Aboriginal community three hundred miles away, more than sixteen days of walking. I ask Birgit, who lives in Croydon, to do me the favor of finding someone headed toward Hells Gate to drop off a package that I've filled with high-energy food. If my plan works, a little food will be waiting for me halfway there. For the moment, my mission is to cover the maximum amount of ground possible. On August 29, 2012, I make camp next to one of the branches of the Albert River. At dawn, I get back on the dusty, red-dirt path and, with awe, discover the "morning glory."[8] I'm incredibly lucky to have seen it.

I start my day with good energy. It's still early when a little head lifts its nose up in the air and sets out across the path, its body stretching on and on, seemingly never-ending. I stand there, openmouthed, excitement running through my veins: it's a magnificent olive python, *Liasis olivaceus*, that's crossing the path. It must be between eleven and thirteen feet long. I put down all my gear and observe it close up, perhaps a bit too close, since he turns around and, slowly raising himself up, retracts his head and part of his upper body to make a "Z." He inspects the air with his tongue; I'm fascinated. Around us, there's no sound, it's just the two of us, him and me. When he moves forward, his skin creates an optical effect that surpasses all movement that occurs in our civilized world. Strangely, I fall in love all over again with this mysterious creature that defies the laws of movement; it had already happened once, ten years ago. I'm practically hypnotized by its slow and efficient locomotion. He's so long and takes so much time to cross the path. . . . He's coming back from the river, at least half a mile below.

In nature, it's imperative to get up very early. This morning is a particular day that promises authentic encounters. It's magical to be witness to a scene of animal life against a backdrop of

---

8. The morning glory is a rare meteorological phenomenon that manifests as a single, sausagelike formation of clouds, which can stretch to over six hundred uninterrupted miles long.

pure nature. I'm going far from the world and from the laws that govern it. I'm going into Aboriginal territory.

I avoid the community of Doomadgee, which is set back a ways. I don't want anyone to see where I'm going. That night, I camouflage myself beneath a large eucalyptus that's on the ground. During the night, I hear wild horses galloping in a frenzy, and Aborigines shouting and fighting. One morning, very early, on this dusty track far from Sutton Creek, a pickup truck pulls up next to me. Inside is a cowboy with a serene face.

"My God, what are you doing here?"

"I'm walking." I smile.

After a silence, he continues, "What are you doing all alone? What do you think about while you're walking here in the middle of nowhere, so far from everything?"

"Well, this morning, I saw an incredible little grey insect with an elongated body, but which was less than an inch long. I'd never seen one like it. When I watched it making its hole, it stopped short, and when it felt me coming closer, it stuck its head in the sand. Then, after a moment, it went back to digging. But when I bent down again, it turned over and played dead. Incredible!"

The cowboy in the black hat smiles without saying a word. Then, "Do you want some water?"

"Yes, I'd love some."

"Oh . . . actually, I see that I'm all out! That was stupid of me . . . Alright, well, good luck with your insects and all the rest."

I watch him drive away slowly so as not to kick up dust. At the same time, in my head, I'm saying, *I can't believe I talked to him about an insect playing dead. My God, he must have thought I was completely crazy.* I giggle and turn a little more toward the west.

I'm surrounded by tall trees with rough skin the color of ocher and ivory, but also by pandanus, which discreetly appear here and there on the banks of the streams I cross. Small, shallow creeks present themselves. I take advantage and refresh myself a little without wanting to soak in them. Today, I'm impatient to get to my water source. I'm hoping to spend the hottest hours of the day there, now that the temperature has risen so high as to flirt with 104°F. I can make out the green line weaving in and out of the red path I've been following for days. "There it is, my little creek," I think. I arrive tired, ready for my break with a good cup of tea in the shade. I put down my bag on the little sandy spur, half shaded and half in sun, when suddenly a magnificent snake over six feet long darts off, vigorously undulating. It's lemon yellow and green, with blue on its back. A shot of adrenaline races through my body, I've never seen a snake like that before. I practically sat on it. Also, it's not the time of day for snakes to be out. But it turns out that it's a green tree snake, *Dendrelaphis punctulatus*, a breed that's active during the day and sleeps at night, very unusual for snakes in Australia. And apparently, it's hardly venomous, or even not at all.

I started using my hammock when I left Burketown. It's super light and covered with a mosquito net, which allows me to rest and recuperate in peace, sheltered from the cloud of flies that follows me. I fall asleep thinking that I should be more careful in the future, especially on the banks of streams. Where there's water, that means there are frogs, and frogs are a delicacy for snakes. In turn, these pythons and water snakes attract other predators such as crocodiles. For this reason, at night, I don't sleep near streams or other sources of water if I can avoid it. The following days, I run into other snakes and incredible birds like the rainbow bee-eater, *Merops ornatus*, which lands just three feet from my tent.

This part of Australia is still preserved, far from tourist centers or other attractions that you'd find on the cover of a tourism brochure. Australia is made for those who love the bush, nature in its raw and violent form, as it can often be out here. My long days of solitude are interspersed with giant trucks with double trailers full of live cattle. I hear them from far away, and have just enough time to leave my cart on the side of the road and to run into the bush to avoid the enormous cloud of red dust that their passage kicks up. This red powder already permeates all my gear, including my toothbrush. In the early afternoon, I enter an environment that takes me by surprise. Gorgeous red rocks seem to greet the traveler. I put down my things, follow a little path, and start to explore these rocks. I climb all over them and, in the back, discover a tree half-strangled by rusty metal wire. It's suffering, part of it has already died off. I promise it that I'll do what I can, and move away. I start in on the descent that leads to Hells Gate. It feels good to arrive somewhere, even if it doesn't amount to much—just a fuel pump in front of an old counter, and rusty old-fashioned things all around. A plot of land adjacent to the restrooms provides a place to set up my tent for the night. The owner announces that someone left a package for me. I'm relieved, it's my food. Now I won't have to ration myself, and I'll even be able to take a day off, which I do the next day. I also take showers, in the big brick building with the metal roof that also contains the bathrooms. On the sun-faded door, a sign reads "Put down the toilet cover after use, otherwise the snakes get in!"

I settle in behind the building with my tent, next to Tom, the only other person on this dusty bit of ground. Tom came here by bike. He's very nice, and we chat about the availability of water on our respective paths. I get up to buy a ginger beer, which isn't a beer, but in Australia is a fermented drink made from ginger. I've been dreaming about it. As I'm paying, I notice someone in the doorway. "Finally!" he exclaims. "You certainly took your time! How long have you been here?"

He's backlit, and all I can see is a silhouette wearing a cowboy hat. But I recognize his voice—it's the cowboy I met several days ago.

"I just got here. And you? What are you doing here?"

"I came to buy cattle, but one of my trailers came off and I've got to repair it. Have to go help my boys, I just wanted to welcome you. See you tonight!"

I look at the owner. "'See you tonight?' What does he mean?" She observes me with a distant air and goes into the back of the store. I find Tom and tell him the whole story. He laughs, but I'm not laughing. So I ask, "Can you chaperone me for the evening?" I know how it can go with these kinds of people in these kinds of places, far from everything. Things can go downhill very quickly, anything is possible. . . .

Night comes, and folks trickle in from all over. Tom stays by my side until he's too tired from his day of nonstop effort. Both of us are used to going to bed early. But this night, it's amid the noises of bipeds partying that we retire to our respective tents. At dawn, everyone's left, they're all headed back to wherever they're going. I wait until Tom's ready, then accompany him to the path, wishing him good luck. As for me, the night before, I made a deal with the cowboy. It consisted of going with him to help him get his cows back in the trailer. In return, I want two of his cows to be spared from going to the slaughterhouse. "It's a deal," he'd said, grasping my hand with his rough paw.

He's there, waiting with the rest of his team where we'd agreed to meet. Everyone gets in, and we drive out to the place. After an afternoon in the dust, the whole team is returned to the campsite. I choose this moment to ask him to drive me to my tree behind the red rocks. By truck, it's just a few gear shifts away. I ask him to bring wire cutters. He tells me that everything is in the metal box in back. He follows me without asking any questions, and when I ask him to cut the metal ties binding my tree, he does it without a word. Silently, we go back to the car. Country music escapes from the speakers, parrots chatter in the high branches, the sun is now gently warm. He takes out a cigarette and lights it, the end of the day is sweet. It feels to me like he's driving fast, but in reality he isn't at all. My perspective from walking is just different. That night, we'll end the day around a fire. He doesn't bring up the favor I asked of him. But there's now a bond between us, written there in the silence. His mute presence by my side seems at once familiar and strange.

The next day, I pack up in the early light of a new day. I head into the bush, which I'm eager to get back to; I have a long crossing in front of me. The midday heat is now inescapable, water sources aren't always viable, as certain streams are already dry, according to the valuable information Tom gave me, and forty miles of soft sand awaits. The days are endless. The heat and physical effort empty me of my precious water. I can't do more than three hundred yards without stopping, so great is the effort required to move my cart in this soft sand. After the third day, Gary from Westmoreland Station brings me a plastic bottle full of water that he'd put in the freezer. It's a huge ice cube that I pass over my entire body as soon as he turns his back. Diane and Gary are bush people, the likes of which they just don't make anymore.

The days pass and my feet tread once again on solid ground before crossing the Calvert River. I finally find a bit of rhythm and joy in walking again. The Calvert River is fortunately not too deep, I'm able to cross it with the water just up to my knees. It's fairly wide; looking at it carefully, you can imagine its strength and its volume during the rainy season. I walk up the ramp on the opposite bank and find an idyllic campsite just to the right. I settle in. A few hours later, a run-down vehicle shows up. An agitated-looking young man gets out, I think I saw him at Hells Gate. He doesn't seem to be in a normal state of mind. Then he takes off without a word. Now I can't stay here, I'm going to have to leave. It was all too bizarre. And how surprising that on this deserted track, the only vehicle to be seen causes me problems. I make a cup of tea and decide to head back into the bush. But here's a pickup coming down the little path leading to my campsite. I grab my things as fast as I can, ready to bolt, when I recognize the driver. It's the cowboy from Hells Gate! He's dropped off his animals and is now headed north to buy others. He says he heard talk of wild cattle, and he'd like to see that with his own eyes. Meanwhile, he takes out an ice chest full of good things. I take advantage of his presence to ask him to watch over the campsite. I want to go wash down below, where no one will be nosing around.

"You're crazy! There are tons of crocodiles in this river."

"Just watch the camp, I'll handle the rest."

Crocodiles almost always attack according to a precise plan of action. Rule number 1: Don't return to the same spot. I get completely undressed far from any eyes at the water's surface, but who knows what's watching from under the water! I don't dawdle. What bliss . . . I come back dripping wet (I don't have a towel, it's too bulky to cart around) and barefoot. At the camp-site, a pretty little fire is burning and the billy is on the fire. Well, it looks like I have a roommate for the night. I tell him about the appearance of the young man in the campsite. "For tonight it won't be a problem, but after that?"

He tells me that he'd bought a pack of soda and explains that his plan is to drop two cans in each creek I'll meet up with, always putting the cans to my left as I approach the creek. It's ingenious, and I'll certainly be very impatient to get to the next creek to find two cold cans in the water. His organization impresses me. He's just as you would imagine a cowboy: silent, eyes lost in the flames of a gently burning fire. In the morn-ing, he rolls up his swag[9] and leaves very early. From now on, I hide each night and avoid the pretty campsites. I share my nights with large wild pigs that I observe with my headlamp. Then in the morning, I leave them a few almonds on the ground as apology. I like hearing them sniff around on the ground so close to my tent. They don't seem to suspect my presence. Wild horses, called brumbies, regularly visit my camp. Kangaroos come back, but are timid, a sign that they're hunted. Snakes slip through the tall grasses as soon as they sense the vibration of

_____

9. Australian version of a sleeping bag.

my steps. Six miles from the Aboriginal community of Nar-
winbi, shacks already rise out of the bush, and even more along
the stream.

I arrive in Borroloola with 195 miles under my belt since I
left Hells Gate. I'll be able to load up on food here. I sit down
outside and enjoy some ice cream, barefooted children with little dogs at their heels amble past. In front of the store, beneath
an acacia tree, some Aborigines are assembled. A group of people suddenly forms a cortege, others join them. There's been a
death. The Aborigines here aren't anything like those I met in
the Great Sandy Desert. Here, alcohol is more dangerous than
cyclones. The faces are swollen, it makes me sad and I move
away. They watch me leave with a disinterested air. At the gas
station, filling the fuel bottle for my stove, they tell me what
goes on at night by the river.

It happens when the tambourines ring out. They tie a dog to
a tree and frenetically bang the tambourines. Meanwhile, an
Aborigine is hung by his feet from a cord controlled by an ac-
complice and attached high up in the same tree. Without waiting long, a monstrous crocodile comes out of the river, excited
by the panic of the dog who sees it coming toward him. The
dog is sacrificed, the scene is quick and unjust. As for the man
hanging head down, they lower him until he can touch the
crocodile's back with his hands, then quickly pull him back up.
I can't believe my ears!

A policeman tells me the same story, adding that they've
intervened and the practice is now forbidden. He explains that
the Aborigines habituated the crocodile by feeding it live dogs
that they threw from the bridge. I shiver. "The bridge that I
crossed at the entrance to the village?"

"Yep, that's the one. And what worries us is that one day the crocodile will confuse a child for a dog. . . ."

I leave this place and return to the bush. I have 296 miles to cover before reaching the next cluster of houses where I'll be able to resupply. I leave the road after sixteen miles and set out towards the northwest. Finally! I can't take any more of this place! Everything is once again silent. I find my rhythm. I notice that in my internal monologue I appropriate things, surely to make them more familiar. For example, when I talk about the bush, I often say, "my bush country." Because for me, where I feel most fully myself, I'm at home. I don't need things or a house. But I need the wilderness. Its sounds, its scents are part of me always, even when I'm not there. To find myself there again is a greater joy each time, even with my tired body and the extreme temperatures. I wouldn't trade places with anyone.

A bit on guard, I anticipate meeting the wild water buffalo. They're said to charge straight ahead as soon as they see a human. The Aborigines are afraid of them and the whites don't enter their territory without a firearm. For me, it's different; I don't have a rifle and I don't know the buffalo. So, I await my first encounter with them to see what it's like.

They arrive late morning, a few days later. From behind my sunglasses I spot one. He's motionless in the bush next to a large eucalyptus. I decide not to look at him. I hum a sweet tune that prevents him from lying in wait, wondering what I'll do next, as he can easily locate me. I don't turn my head, I stay calm (it's primordial, since if an animal senses fear, it will charge) and above all, I repeat the same gestures at the same speed. He doesn't move from his post. Over the following days, I spot enormous buffalo excrements that are taller than bull or cow pies. I also find lots of tracks.

I make camp in the middle of the bush on earth composed of a grass that grows in tufts. I tamp down the grass and put up my tent. The evening is cool, finally, after a day where the temperature rose to over 100°F. I leave the vestibule of my tent open and press my nose against the door's mosquito netting. The night is magical, blue-black, the stars glittering with an unusual luminosity. Everything is calm, and I sink into a well-deserved sleep. Suddenly, in the middle of the night, still lying on my back I open my eyes: a subtle sound reaches my ears, "*Shuuss . . . shuss . . . shuuuusss . . .*" Then nothing. Through the mesh of my tent everything is grey. I realize that I'm gazing at the belly of a buffalo. The color is mouse grey, the form is round. I stay calm, not moving a millimeter. Neither does he. Part of his body is gently resting against my tent. How long will he stay there? I feel him sniff the air, then "*shuuss, shussss*" and "*repfutttt, repfutttt.*" He tears out the tufts of tall, dry grass, exhaling as he eats, making these distinct sounds. He eats peacefully. His movements are almost silent. And it turns out that I like him, he doesn't seem dangerous to me. I will find them by the dozens, killed by helicopter here and there. I'm sad and angry—man is in denial and won't look for real solutions. He eliminates problems that will only pop back up like mushrooms. They can get a dingo to eat meat laced with mortal poison (*poison 1080*), which causes an agonizing death. They shoot camels in central Australia, or sometimes wild pigs, from helicopters. In Europe, we did the same thing with foxes, which we nearly eliminated until someone realized that we needed to protect them instead because there was an invasion of mice, which the fox used to eat! Can't we put in place a systemic sterilization adapted to remote wilderness, something that the animal can eat that can be dropped by helicopter? Killing them like weeds isn't a solution. A life is a life.

I see a cloud of dust before me; I hear the sound of hoofs against earth, I'm guessing cattle. An Aborigine on horseback approaches wearing a cowboy hat and flip-flops. His English is perfect. Frank owns a cattle station by the name of "Seven Emus" where he hosts people to share his culture, the earth, and the importance of tradition. He has a hard time understanding that I'm walking alone and sleeping in the bush. "You must've seen some amazing things after all this time in all these countries? Even us, we only sleep in the bush from time to time," he guffaws, eyes widening. We chat for more than an hour about life, plants, the importance of educating young people—and the bush, of course. "I think the world needs people like you so that the Earth continues to turn," he tells me. His voice is low and serious. I smile.

I walk through a camp where Aboriginal men are keeping watch around a fire, while the young people gather their horned livestock. I arrive in Butterfly Springs. The rock carefully collects rainwater that fills its basin on the eastern side, while sand forms a beach on the west. It's a water hole situated amid ancient eucalyptus trees launching themselves towards the sky. I let myself fall into this sweet water entirely clothed. Isolated from everything, my head in the clouds, I soak up this paradise. The sunset paints the rock an unforgettable earthy red-orange. I set up camp and return to bathe, this time naked in the middle of the night. The moon has just appeared above the rock wall, beautiful and full. I revel in the water and rediscover deeper instincts, feeling a connection to something bigger than I am. It's pure beauty. I let myself float a bit more, watching the stars, and decide to return to camp four hundred yards away. I remain barefoot. I turn on my headlamp and move forward in the soft sand, between the bushes. Abruptly, in the beam of my headlamp, I catch two magnificent white snakes with light brown zigzags, their heads undulating above the sand. I'm so lucky to see them, even from five feet away and barefoot (oops!). A cat-eyed gecko licks its chops a few feet from my tent. I find it deeply stirring, the isolation of this place allows nature and animals to breathe and to blossom. With regret, I retire until dawn.

The rest of my steps will be nothing more than managing the heat in relation to my available energy. I'm getting better and better at coping with this humidity that's become palpable. The air is heavy, stifling. I hear dingos shouting during the night. I like feeling that they're not far away, as water's getting scarce. I arrive opposite Ngukurr, an Aboriginal community that lives on the other side of the wide Roper River. I make camp high up on the bank. Crocodiles patrol the opposite bank—I can see them without binoculars. I haven't seen a vehicle in days, but the cloud of dust on the horizon indicates that one is approaching. I stay hidden below, and a few minutes later the vehicle comes back the other way, this time close by. It's the cowboy from Hells Gate with one of his friends, they followed the tracks of my cart to find me. They're on their way to Doomadgee, where they'll fly over the Wall of China, a magnificent rock formation, by helicopter. They join my camp, roast steaks on the coals while I treat myself to the eggs they gave me. The ambiance has changed, the silent cowboy becomes a true cowboy once again. I take advantage of it to slip away into the night, to my tent. Before dawn, I'm awakened by a gunshot. The guy I've never seen before has a pistol in his hand and is yelling, "Get up! Coffee's ready!" *Bunch of lunatics . . .*

Daylight hasn't yet returned. The fire is nothing more than a pile of embers. I learn that they slept with their guns for fear of crocodiles.

"You're just a bunch of little girls, aren't you!"

"Do you know the story of the Calvert River?" asks the second cowboy.

"No, tell me!" (I move away from the fire to hear him better, since he has an accent from the center of Queensland that you could cut with a knife.)

"You saw a guy in your camp, a fidgety guy with an old truck?"

"Yeah."

"So, before coming to see you, he shot at a helicopter that was mustering cattle nearby."

"No!"

"Yep. There are some strange folks around here, you should watch out."

I watch the silent cowboy whose eyes are fixed on the coals. He finally opens his mouth. "She's alright, she knows what she's doing. Don't you know where she's come from? Even we couldn't have made it without horses. I've seen it!"

That morning we exchange addresses and phone numbers, because it's certainly the last time that we'll see each other on this path. I'm about to leave their territory. A green snake chooses to zigzag toward our bare feet. The silent cowboy jumps back while the other insists on catching it. "I don't like those things!" he declares, getting up.

The signal to leave is given, and they go, leaving me with food that will be an enormous help as I make my way to Mataranka, 143 miles away. I wish them a good trip and ask them to give my best regards to their families. The friend waves from his open window.

Two days later, my trail joins up with a larger path. My cart jounces over the large pebbles on the roadside, but from here on out I'm heading west. Everything is to my advantage, the sun will be at my back until noon, so I walk without lifting my head much and set targets I have to reach every hour that slips by. Then comes the rain. I'm geared up and walking, and still it holds me back. Rain is capable of slowing down time. Its smell alone makes you want to put down roots—no matter where you happen to be—and never leave. This morning, that's what it does to me. I unzip my tent's rainfly and see a bird gripping a tree trunk on the side opposite the direction in which the rain's falling. Like me, he's waiting for the right moment. The rains are already here, I need to get back to Darwin before the monsoons become too strong.

Three days from the resupply point where Gregory is waiting for me, I'm again lucky enough to come across wild donkeys. They're just too cute, and extremely curious: I surprise more than one hiding behind a tree to better observe me. The encounter gives me new energy. I arrive exhausted, gaunt, and covered in a layer of red dust, smelling of effort to boot. Gregory is there with all the necessary equipment, news from Switzerland, and a few surprises. *Yes!*

I'm happy to see Gregory, to speak French and to share my meals; I take advantage of having water nearby to soak my legs often. I sleep and recuperate. We spend an entire day meticulously preparing my pack. Everything needs to be washed and my camp stove needs to be fixed. In the meantime, I give telephone interviews with Switzerland, I send postcards, and the last day, I write a newsletter that Gregory will send. It turns out that I didn't really have time to do nothing. It's already the end of the resupply, and Gregory leaves. . . . *Thank you, thank you* . . .

The last section until Darwin (Adelaide River[10]) is nothing but pure effort, and from here on out, people are practically everywhere. I have to manage the end-of-day rainstorms that clear the stifling air. Torrents of water fall from the sky, and it almost makes me think of Mongolia. I use my hammock. If I want to avoid getting drenched, it's easier to suspend myself and to use the waterproof top cover than to put up my tent. The landscape is now tropical with palm trees, pandanus, tall green grasses, and climbing plants. All this green contrasts with the landscape of the previous weeks, during my crossing of the east and the Arnhem Land Region. Here, everything is lush, the green glistens beneath the welcome rain. The birds frolic in the high branches, chattering away, the kangaroos pretend to tolerate all this water. I get to my destination, the Adelaide River, with a smile that stretches from ear to ear. It's just before the storm, beneath a blazing sun. I'm so happy, I did it! It's as though all the energy has just left my body. I get to Darwin, a hotel room has been reserved under my name from Switzerland. I'm exhausted! *Please do not disturb.*

---

10. The Adelaide River is my stopping point. It's here where the commotion of the city of Darwin begins, and the traffic makes walking on the highway too dangerous. I had a bad experience when I tried to do this entering Chiang Mai, Thailand.

12. Southern Australia

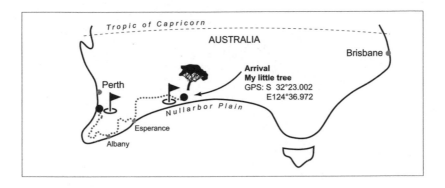

I visit the doctor's office

NORTHERN AUSTRALIA IS UNDER WATER, THE RAINY season is in full swing. I'm in Perth, in the west. I can't seem to recuperate the way I'd like. Once again I barely made it through my period, which completely knocked me out. Since this morning, I've been trying to make an appointment to have some blood tests done. First I have to establish myself as the patient of a generalist, who then sends me to a lab. Eight hundred dollars later I get the results. I'm just a little low on iron, everything else is in good shape. I'm almost surprised by how good the lab report is. The doctor's diagnosis is a generalized fatigue of the body, the consequence of my physical efforts of the past two and a half years. So I decide to go to plan B. I'll have to help my body the way I know how: I'll get massages with an osteopath once a day for the time my preparations here will take.

I enter a store I know well at 900 Hay Street. They sell only topographic maps. I leave smiling, maps tucked under my arm— I'm feeling better already. I stop at the health food store where I buy spirulina, acerola vitamin C, cold-pressed oil, magnesium and calcium pills, organic almond butter, energizing tea, omega-3 gel caps, iron pills, and still more. I also take the opportunity to buy myself some mangos, avocados, lemons, bananas, sprouted grains. . . . I also find packets of coffee-flavored energy booster. All of it is organic, free of insecticide, free of preservatives or any other additives. My plan, "I set out in great shape," is launched.

Bibbulmun Track, here I am again

I've decided to follow Bibbulmun Track[11] south, which will keep me from worrying about water and allow me to focus on managing my physical effort and adapting it to my condition. I know this 620-mile path well. I come here before every expedition to train and to test my gear's effectiveness. I've walked it in both directions many times. I'll follow it with pleasure, but don't let that make you think that it will require any less effort. There are few people on it, most of the time I'll be alone.

But this night, as darkness falls, the sound of footsteps rises on the night air. The blanket of dried eucalyptus leaves helps me to hear. I'm in my tent, which I've set up beneath the shelter

---

11. Bibbulmun Track, made by volunteers, is a path that threads its way through the bush. See bibbulmuntrack.org.au

of a tarp that gathers water and channels it into a reservoir in back. The footsteps come closer, and from where I am I can see sweaty skin and the top of a backpack. The biped ducks under the shelter and puts down his belongings. I stifle an "Oh my God!" without being able to keep myself from laughing. It's a man in his prime, built with pectorals clearly visible and well-defined, and a perfectly hairy chest. Yet, his face is deeply marked by sun and by life, and that's all I'll say about it, except that he hurries to put his clothes back on, or to just put them on at all. He shyly apologizes, "I didn't think there'd be anyone at the campsite." Now I can't sleep. I decide to make some tea. I watch him set up camp, careful not to miss any gesture that would show him to be the hiker he doesn't look like he is. For starters, he's missing some teeth. It's the distinctive sign of the tumultuous life of a fighter, maybe even prison time, or simply a lack of money to replace them. I keep up my guard. He explains that he practically lives on this 620-mile trail, that he only leaves it to visit his aging father and to resupply. "Just now, I was on the beach and lost track of time, but I decided to leave to spend the night here because there's a storm coming up." He shakes his head and murmurs, "I should have left earlier!"

I don't remember his name, but I remember the story he told me by the light of his headlamp.

A snake and a turquoise beach

On a summer's afternoon, he had just arrived at the idyllic little beach on William Bay, below the campsite. It's a section of the path that follows the coast. The beach is protected by magnificent round rocks. The water is a crystal blue and cool—a dream after a day of walking. So he went for a swim and even fell asleep there. A lover of beaches, he often stays on them until late and, depending on the season, happily sleeps on them. The next day, he woke up early and continued his route along the Bibbulmun. And this is what happened three days later: he was camping with another hiker who had run out of bandages for his blisters, so he offered to give him some. Chatting away, he stuck his hand unsuspectingly in his first-aid kit and, without realizing it right away, took out . . . a snake almost five feet long, which he dropped in a movement of silent terror. It wasn't just any snake, but a western tiger snake, *Notechis scutatus occidentalis*. It's a species that I find beautiful, robed in black matte with a yellow belly. But it's also extremely venomous.

What terrified my neighbor the most was the fact that he'd toted this snake around in his pack for three days without knowing it. Anything could have happened in that span of time.

"Yes," I say, "including that it could have left your pack while it was in your tent. . . ."

"Back then, I didn't have a tent, but since this happened I always sleep on the beach in my tent. It must have crawled into my pack during the night since, on the beach where I was, it's a bit chilly at night."

I drink my tea and look at him. He's still visibly shaken.

After two months of walking while carrying my only backpack, I had to leave the Bibbulmun to go see an osteopath. The sixty-five pounds on my back have aggravated an old injury. I can't get my cart again until Albany, where it's waiting for me. Before then, I encounter two forest fires, snakes and more snakes, then finally get back to the sea and its eternal enemy, the sand dunes.

I wake up early, near four o'clock in the morning, well before the bush comes to life; this allows me to see the kangaroos in ecstasy before the sunrise and to surprise the blue wren in the undergrowth. They're little birds with turquoise blue feathers. I never tire of watching or, even more important to me, of feeling nature awaken. I draw from it the energy that heals my invisible wounds. I make sure that my walk is accompanied by magnificent animal encounters. We often neglect the mental aspect of things, the connection between body and spirit. My encounters and the communion I have with nature nourish me in a different way. Caring for my body also includes the psychological. So I work at it . . . I stop as many times as it wants, drink as many teas as it desires . . . and still cover the distance. I wish for everyone one day to walk Bibbulmun Track. There's no better way to explore this land.

I arrive in Albany where a big surprise is waiting for me—my mom made the trip. I haven't seen her in over two and a half years.

"I'm sick of your adventures, so I'm coming out there!" she tells me, laughing, on the phone. My mom is the woman who has inspired me the most in my life. I'm wildly lucky to have been born into that middle-class household in the heart of the

Swiss Jura mountains. We reunite with great emotion, it's been so long.

During her stay in Albany, we don't stop laughing and eating good Swiss chocolate. I see her in a new light: she's in a universe different from her own. I take indescribable pleasure watching her evolve in different situations. One day, when we're in a clearing ringed by beautiful pines, she has her packet of cookies stolen by a kangaroo! I can't believe it, I've never seen anything like it! In just a short little while, surrounded by nature, she sees all the birds imaginable, but also dolphins, still more kangaroos, and even a mama quokka, *Setonix brachyurus*, with her little one, which is very rare here. It's not her first trip to Australia, though. She came with my brother, who was responsible for my resupplies during my 2002–2003 Australian expedition. The first morning she was here, she disappeared! Extremely worried, my brother and I left immediately to look for her. We found her over a mile from camp, sitting on a plastic chair in front of a little shop, a cup of coffee in her hand. I asked her what she was doing there.

"Can't you see I'm having my coffee? You know I always like my coffee in the morning." Laughter erupts and takes over for a moment.

"Alright, so tell me, just for fun, how exactly did you order your coffee?" (She doesn't speak a word of English.)

"I said, 'café café.'" My brother and I are now sitting and we've ordered . . . coffee.

"But wait, did you really walk all the way here?"

"Of course!" she answered, her tone very serious.

The moment for us to part ways comes much too soon. She

helps me buy what I need and it's already time for me and my cart to head off toward my little tree, which isn't so far away now. See you very soon, my sweet mother.

Two feet, one handle . . .

It's the beginning of the month of April, which means it's the start of winter. This region of Australia is exposed to the ocean's whims, and I withstand them day after day in the hope that the next day will be soothed by a ray of sunlight that will dry my belongings. But none of that happens. The cold of the sea steals onto the land, accompanied by gusts of rain. At the end of the first week, my body has already had enough.

I camouflage myself beneath the branches, not to keep from getting wet, but so as not to hear the sound of the rain against my tent. It's driving me crazy. The damp is seeping into my body and is giving me cramps. In the middle of the path, my cart gets stuck in the mud. I try to get it out, but the handle snaps and comes off. The rain courses down my face. I stop with one cart handle in my hand. It's time to do something! I find some boards that must have been used as part of a shelter for a tractor or something like it.

I take over the place, in two minutes I've put up my tent, keeping it dry. I stay there, drinking tea and watching the rain fall. I consider, and realize I don't have a choice—I'm going to have to continue with just one handle.

At the entrance to Esperance, I turn around to see a sign that reads "Albany 483 km" (300 miles). I've completed half of that route with just one handle. I'm as focused as when you pass the finish line of a race. I'm not stopping until I'm in front of a motel on the seashore, which doesn't take long to appear. I leave my cart outside, remove my backpack that's now just a sponge, take off my Gore-Tex jacket that's dripping everywhere, smooth my hair a bit and open the door, hoping that they won't refuse me a room. Despite my exhausted state, I smile. The girl behind the front desk is wonderful, she gives me a room with a bathtub. Without asking what I'm doing, she points me in the direction of room 23. I go in, put down my things, undress and go directly into the shower, which is piping hot. I just stand there beneath this water, without thinking. After an eternity, I slowly wash with the array of products that the hotel has provided. I wrap myself in the big towel and draw a bath. I change my mind, I won't be able to wait. Completely naked, hair still wet, I slide between the clean sheets.

I'm awakened the next morning at eleven o'clock by the cleaning lady. I turn over and fall back asleep until five o'clock that evening. . . . When I open my eyes, I'm ravenous.

After a second night, I start to feel better. But my muscles worry me. I continue to take homeopathic doses of magnesium and arnica. I walk to the industrial zone, in my pocket is the address of a guy who solders aluminum. I have terrible pain in my back, to the point where I have to stop walking and lie down in the grass on the side of the road. I leave my two handles with this magician, who promises my cart will be good as new in two days. With one look he sees the state I'm in, and offers to have his apprentice drive me back to town. I gratefully accept. I lie down on my bed and call Switzerland.

We have to synchronize the photographer, cameraman, and helicopter pilot for my arrival. They want an exact date. . . . I promise to call Gregory back soon, as I'm in no state to make a decision.

Two days later, I take the same road north again. The solderer thought it would be nice to make the two handles the same height, so he also cut the handle that was in good shape, then reinforced the whole thing.

I set out again, I feel like I've been beaten up. Everything hurts, and pushing my cart with two hands, I realize that doing it with just one, I twisted my body a bit. As a result, my body resorted to using muscles that it hadn't in almost three years. This explains my current state. But it gets worse. I realize that with the shorter handles, my position pushing the cart isn't at all the same as before.

On the other hand, after three days of walking the sun reappears and stays with me, to my great pleasure. It's back after the rain, which causes an explosion of colors and forms in the bush that I watch unfold and open up before my eyes. From candy pink to shimmering red to yellow . . . I can't believe it, my favorite eucalyptus are in bloom. I'm euphoric.

What's incredible about the process of accumulating years in your life is that at certain moments, in precise circumstances, you might relive things or see people again that you've already seen. When I walked across this region ten years ago, I fell in love with these trees with the glistening, copper-colored trunks. They change colors depending on the time of day and the season. At night their bark is red, while at dawn it's copper, almost green. It's definitely a eucalyptus, its name is *Eucalyptus salmonophloia.* I feast my eyes on it. It calms me to find this realm again.

In the morning, it takes a long time before my muscles are able to function very well. It's almost like having to relearn how to walk. With my first steps of the day, my legs haven't yet calculated the distance to the ground, giving the impression that I'm somewhat robotic. It's imperative that I warm up my body before leaving. I do a few yoga poses, gently stretching. And I exclaim, "I'm going to make it! I'm going to make it!" I talk to my body. "You're going to have to keep going." There are 185 miles left.

Months ago, I made the decision not to have folks from Switzerland come to my arrival. I want to reach my tree, that's all, without fuss or euphoria. Just my tree. For a long time that wasn't my vision, then I wanted to have things happen as simply as possible, and now I just want to enjoy a sunset with my tree. My expedition leader told me, "Well, it's your choice." But I clearly felt a small moment of heartache. Today I know that it's the right decision. I advance in the direction of my little tree, this same tree I slept beneath so many years ago, during my 2002–2003 expedition, when I was with my dog, D'Joe.

It's the end of the day, I enter the town of Norseman, which marks the end of this long plain that connects Australia from the south to the west and what they call Nullarbor Plain. I rent a small room and get to work: I need to advise the technical participants, because my point of arrival is far from everything and I have to confirm the date. As usual I'm going to do all this with my little BlackBerry. I receive lots of messages of encouragement from people I don't even know. Over the years, it's something I've always found extraordinary. I thank each and every one of you who have followed me and supported me. I quickly take care of the logistics and spend the rest of the time in the shower. My muscles ache badly. I get a text message from the cowboy of the north, who says that he'll be passing through, without saying when.

I leave with a strange feeling in my mouth; in certain moments I'm already overcome by nostalgia. I savor each instant, I stop a little more than usual. I let myself be lulled by the whisperings of the bush, small lizards climb on my backpack and clown around. I slip once again a leaf of saltbush, *Atriplex*, under my tongue, a movement I do automatically, no matter where in Australia I am. This leaf has a distinctive surface that's almost imperceptibly velvety. There are more than two hundred kinds of saltbush, of which forty-five are native to Australia. This shrub with its tiny, light grey leaves that have a subtle bluish shine completely stops functioning—if that's the right way of putting it—during periods of serious drought. It plays dead! It comes back to life with the rain or with a little morning dew. I've always admired this little shrub that's not very pretty at first glance and that's one of those elements of the landscape that you don't pay attention to. And yet, it's the ultimate survivor. When you place a single one of its leaves on your tongue, an explosion of salty essence spreads throughout your mouth. It's not really salt, it's more like a grain of salt in its Sunday best, wearing a famous designer's gown. What emerges is as refined and indescribable as soup made from the roots of the tall green stalks you have to tear from the soil. After hours of cleaning, cooking, and blending, the soup is finally ready. At the time I was at a farm in New Zealand where I was working, and it was there that I ate my first Jerusalem artichoke soup. In the face of such an exquisite delicacy, I was learning that food unlocks emotions and tastes that aren't always possible to describe. I still have its sublime taste in my mouth, and it's been more than twenty years.

The saltbush is my point of reference, it's where I turn when everything's going wrong, and water becomes dangerously rare. Even when the soil is devoid of trees, of life, of shade, there's always a saltbush not too far away. Its salt keeps me from losing too much water. Today it's everywhere, it covers the ground, contrasting with the brilliant red eucalyptus trunks that are so beautiful.

I delight in these moments of pure harmony until I'm fewer than sixty miles from my point of arrival. One morning my legs don't want to move anymore, just like that. They tremble uncontrollably by themselves. I massage them, as well as my feet, with the essential oils I have left, and swallow more magnesium. After all this attention, they deign to stop trembling. But what's going on? I'm fewer than sixty miles away! You're not going to give up on me now? I look at my topo map. . . . I'll swing through Balladonia, a popular stop for truckers. Nullarbor Plain isn't inhabited, but there are roadhouses. I barely make it.

I ask for a small room, they give me the key, I pay and go back out. I'm walking like an obese penguin. In front of my belongings, a cowboy is smoking a cigarette. He slowly lifts his eyes from where they're hidden beneath his hat. It's good to see a familiar face! He smiles. "I was in the area, so I looked at the latest news on your Web site. Figured I'd find you around here." He's brought fresh fruit and vegetables. "I thought this would help you in the home stretch. While I was waiting I went to see your little tree. It's still there!" I smile happily. It's a joke that he'd made back up north, with his buddy, around the fire. He'd teased, "And what if your little tree isn't there anymore, what will you do?"

I explain that my legs are on strike. "You'll make it," he says. "I'll resupply you, I've got a week before I have to go to cattle sale." I'm moved by his kindness. I let the profoundly restorative water of a shower run over my body and I talk to my legs. I stretch them, massage them, until I fall, exhausted, on the bed. I look out through the open door, I hear the bush murmur, it's not far. I'm already feeling the first pangs of separation. I already miss the bush, before I've even left it. I get dressed in time to join the man in the hat for dinner. I still can't believe he's here, I'm so pleased.

The bar serves as dining room and you can only order whatever the cook (if you can call him that) has decided to put on the menu. I retire when the guys at the bar start tossing back beers. I need to sleep.

The next day I wake up very early. I massage my legs and take another hot shower, which does them good. And then I set off. It takes hours before they function more or less normally. I don't stop, I can't take the risk of my legs stiffening up. Around 1 p.m., a vehicle passes me and stops in front of me. It's him, the man in the hat, as I call him. I smile. He's brought hot coffee and fruit, but also a fresh pancake. I feast.

When it's time to get going, my legs won't move and I'm in incredible pain! I say aloud, "I don't believe it, you walk for almost three years and now you can't get me to my tree? I hope you're joking!"

The cowboy looks at me strangely. "So you're talking to your legs, is that it?"

"Oh, you, not now! I'm sure that you talk to your balls!"

He laughs like he'll never be able to stop and I, exhausted, do the same. Alone, I continue to walk until twilight, it's so pleasant in the bush as night falls. However, my humor turns downright sour when I see him far ahead, on the side of the road. I push a little farther and catch up to him. "What do you think you're doing here?"

"Do you think I'm going to leave you in this state in the bush?" he retorts. He attaches an empty orange juice bottle to a tree, like they do in the north. "I've reserved a room and a meal for you at the roadhouse." Then he adds, "You'll never make it there in this state, do you know how many kilometers you've got left? Your legs are going to give up before you get there. Come on, get in, I'll drop you off at your room and bring you back here at day's first light. You'll be able to take care of your legs, at least. I feel sorry for you, you know! And it takes a lot for me to feel sorry for anyone, believe me."

What if my legs refuse to take me to my tree? I absolutely have to get there. . . .

When I wake up in the little room in the back of the roadhouse, it's still dark. On the steps of the room next door, a cowboy smokes his first cigarette. A steaming cup of coffee is sitting on my stoop. It's been a long time since anyone has made me coffee in the morning. "I made you some coffee, Sleepy-head, you need it." *Thank you, thank you . . .*

In the silence, the night battles with the day as it lifts its groggy head. Then he says, "Departure in fifteen minutes."

I somehow make it out of my room, a dozen road workers in the glow of the new day greet me with "Good morning!" and encouraging applause. I smile, "Thanks, guys!" I crossed their construction site yesterday, they're rebuilding part of the road. We arrive at the empty bottle, which he detaches from the tree. He takes out all my gear, and hands me a hot cup of coffee that he made in anticipation. There are moments in life when words are useless, this is one of them. He helps me so generously. The collective spirit of Australians can be found right here.

The state of my legs doesn't get better, but it doesn't get worse, either. I realize, while studying my map, that my tree is a day and a half away and I only have a day left to walk. I messed up in my calculations. I'm going to have to walk at night to make up for the delay. Suddenly, I realize what this means, and tears run down my cheeks. I'm like a kid in a fit of despair. I'm finally going to arrive at my little tree! All my pains, all my battles flow from my body at this moment. Alone, sitting in the bush, I let my tears tell their story. I think of my dog, D'Joe. . . . I get up, emptied but lighter, a weight has just lifted from my shoulders. I put my pack on my back and throw my-self into this day that, I know, will be interminable and above all, the last one.

My legs now move jerkily, they're fighting, they're giving everything they've got. Meanwhile, at the roadhouse, the cameraman and photographer are received by a man in a black cowboy hat. The helicopter's going to show up three miles before my tree. We even had to figure out how to resupply the helicopter, this place is so far from everything. For the moment, I push into the night that's just begun to fall, the bit of fog that cloaks it is so pretty, creating a soft mood. At dawn, I'm barely standing when the resupply arrives: coffee, pancake. The man in the hat confirms all is well with the cameraman, the photographer, the helicopter. I eat standing up and then I'm off. I'm afraid that my legs will refuse to leave again. I must have an unimaginable quantity of lactic acid in them at this point. I can't go any farther, it's 2 p.m. and I'm three miles from my little tree. I let myself fall to the ground, I'm an hour early. I smile . . . perfect timing! I inhale the bush directly from the ground. I dig a hole, there's something I absolutely must do. Seated, I collect a few twigs, some small branches scattered across the ground, and I light a small fire. I place my teapot on the fire and watch the scene as though hypnotized. It's my last tea, I'm bidding good-bye to the bush, which I miss already.

An hour later, I stand back up and promise my legs that these are the last three miles. I move across this open plain, the purr of a motor can be heard on the horizon. A mile farther on, the helicopter flies over me like a bird of prey ready to swoop down. I can now see my little tree. It hasn't moved, it's as beautiful as ever. My legs astonishingly take flight, the sun is setting behind me, I turn around to see the dazzling show. Five hundred yards away, near my little tree, there are people I've never seen. My eyes don't leave my little tree, as though to help me focus, but I can't help it, tears flow from beneath my sunglasses. I've made it! I touch the bark of my tree with my right hand. "I'm back, darling." I sit down. And I let the emotions pour from my heart.

To think that I once dreamed of this moment!

Acknowledgments

Upon the completion of this book, I would like to thank Loyse Pahud, who corrected the first drafts with respect and rigor. When I wandered a bit too far into my world, she knew how to stop me in time and with diplomacy. My mom was my first reader and, at any hour of the day or night, guided me from the very first chapter with the help of her judicious commentary. Then come the book's graphic creations by Pauline Rochat, whom I thank for her patience, and Janice Lachat, who kindly lent his touch when we were in doubt. Next, the whole team at Michel Lafon who oversaw the smooth development of the book. A very big thanks to Elsa Lafon, who knew how to assist me over several long-distance phone calls during my expedition but, above all, who was able to create a climate of confidence and had the sensitivity to allow me freedom in my approach to the writing and creation of the book. Her confidence was an important ingredient in the completion of this work.

From the bottom of my heart, I wish to thank the people who made it possible for an expedition of this scale to see daylight. I think of the incredible luck I had when I met the founder of Debiopharm, Doctor Rolland-Yves Mauvernay. I didn't yet know that he would be the rock that would permit the birth of the eXplorAsia expedition. With his son, Thierry, they did more than help me financially; they helped me to grow with their advice and support during the most difficult moments. It is with great respect that I thank you to have listened, long ago, to a young woman tell you of her dream, which bore the name "eXplorAsia."

Gaz Naturel was by my side for "The Path of the Andes," and they loyally renewed their sponsorship for this long expedition. I wish to profess my respect and my thanks for the commitment you took on in helping a woman with such an ambitious project.

I warmly thank Mr. Patrick Delarive, who with Whitepod, joined forces with eXplorAsia, and the three principal sponsors of my expedition.

And a big thanks to: TISSOT, FEMINA, Yosemite Lausanne, Air France, Alain Pezzoni, Retripa, Falke, Icebreaker, Flexcell, North Face, Balz and Werner, Radical Design, Garmin, Abonobo, Vélo Couché, and MTL Chaussure.

Also, thanks go to Diane Doyle and Ron Roman (photographers), Jean-Luc Wey (video voice-over), and all those I'm forgetting who have helped me along the way.

And finally, the person who helped me to put this excursion together, who came to meet me for resupplies, and who synchronized this long expedition full of unforeseen circumstances. I am, of course, talking about my expedition leader

Gregory Barbezat, whom I thank from the bottom of my heart.

I was particularly touched by the generosity of the people over the years who helped me bring home my dog, D'Joe. I can't leave out his osteopath, Doctor Mireille Piguet, who offered D'Joe her friendship and helped him to bear old age. And I would like to thank my mom, who accompanied him in the last stage of his life, with all the love in the world, and the respect that this little old man with the mischievous eyes deserved.

I also wish to thank you, who hold my book in your hands, and all those who have followed me over the years. Know that your messages of encouragement have given me tremendous energy in the most challenging moments.

About the Author

Born in Switzerland, Sarah Marquis has travelled the world alone and on foot for twenty-three years, crossing the United States, Australia and South America. She has given more than three hundred talks in French and English, including talks for TED and the Geographical Society and has been profiled in *The New York Times Magazine*. *National Geographic* named Sarah an 'Explorer of 2014'.